The Priest

Ancient Priest of Chichen Itza Reincarnated

By

Julia SvadiHatra

THE PRIEST

Ancient Priest of Chichen Itza Reincarnated

iUniverse books may be ordered through booksellers or by contacting:

iUniverse
1663 Liberty Drive
Bloomington, IN 47403
www.iuniverse.com
1-800-Authors (1-800-288-4677)

ISBN: 978-1-4401-4117-1 (pbk)
ISBN: 978-1-4401-4118-8 (ebk)

Printed in the United States of America

Editor: Roxane Christ www.1steditor.biz

Cover design: Most4u.net

iUniverse rev. date: 11/2/2009

iUniverse, Inc.
New York Bloomington

Dreams
Translated by Olga Lipovskaya

The Priest

1. THEY PULLED MY BODY OUT OF ME, April 25, 1996
2. HIEROGLYPH ON THE PALM, September 12, 1992
3. ATHARVAN, October 13, 1989
4. BABY FROM THE RIVER, April 11, 1992
5. THE UPPER KINGDOM, October 24, 1993
6. THE QUEEN OF A CRYSTAL KINGDOM, December 4, 2007
7. ARABIAN AND AMERICAN MOUNTAINS, (2 pyramids: Egypt and Mexico), October 25, 1990
8. I RETURN TO THE LAND WHERE I LIVED BEFORE, November 23, 1992
9. THE POWER OF THE FOUR, August 21, 1992
10. GREAT HARMONY OF NATURE, October 8, 1991
11. LUMINOUS BODIES OF PLANTS, January 8, 1992
12. SPECTRUM, February 23, 1992,
13. GOD BLESSING, ANGELS, July 20, 1995
14. THE GRAIN OF DIVINITY, January 4, 1992
15. A MESSAGE FROM THE MAGNIFICENT MAYA PEOPLE, June 24, 2008

Dedication

Dedicated to the creativity of the people who lived on Earth or will be living in the future.

Leonardo Da Vinci, Wolfgang Amadeus Mozart, Alexander Pushkin, Johann Sebastian Bach, Tchaikovsky, Lev Tolstoy, *Michelangelo, Rembrandt van Rijn,* George Friedrich Händel, Alfons Ven, "Abba", Elvis Presley, Rimsky Korsakov, *Albert Einstein,* "Enigma", *Galileo Galilee, Nicolaus Copernicus,* Nostradamus, Tesla, Mendeleyev, Marie Curie, Louis Pasteur, Stephen Hawking, *Jan Van Hyusum, Jan Davidsz de Heem, Edward Grieg,* Peter Breughel, Pierre-Auguste Renoir, Frans Snyders, William Shakespeare, conductor Igor Golovchin, actor Jack Nicholson, opera singer Vecheclav Osipov, father of wave genetic P. Gariaev, child prodigy Akiane Kramarik, Connie Talbot ... *you can add any creative person you know...*

Acknowledgements

Thanks to Mr. Jorge Esma Bazan, Director of Patronato Culture, State of Yucatan, Mexico and to his great team for their effort in keeping the architectural complex of Chichen Itza and other historical monuments in Yucatan in excellent, perfect condition. Their highly organized planning and the maintenance of international levels of standards provide the tourists with the wonderful opportunity to enjoy such important events as the "Equinox in Chichen Itza".

Grateful thanks to Wilma Herrada Dodero, who navigated me with good advices, help and support while I was in Yucatan, Mexico.

To dear Alfons Ven who taught me to ask myself: "Who am I?" His genius gave me the unique possibility to return my self and others to our own selves by using his "miracle pills", changing our lives forever. It helped me in opening the doors to a waterfall of my own enormous amount of energy and in staying in great, dynamic health, optimistic and happy.

Special, deeply felt thanks to the wise, Diana Cherry, who, over the last 60 years, has helped thousands of people getting rid of the heavy burden of their past and find out *who* they really were through studying their Spirit Journey and seeing their lives under a new light.

Special thanks to Roxane Christ, my editor, who encouraged and supported me during the writing of this book. With her thorough knowledge of the language, she helped me, and many other authors, bring our books to life and make them available to readers. She put her full attention and kind heart into my book, and it was a great pleasure working with her.

I express special thanks to my ex-husband, Tim Sviridov. I shall acknowledge the massive efforts of laboriously collecting and systematizing the dreams, which are used in this book, as well as for the production of the beautiful covers.

The Priest

Thanks to Carlos Castaneda for the invention of new terminology, which helped me, and many other authors all over the world, to describe the Spirit world. Going through his books, his message became perfectly clear. I guess because of my past life experience as an ancient Maya Priest, I could read between the sentences what was impossible for him to describe or put into words.

Thanks to the wonderful Crystalinks Metaphysical and Science Website which provided with great image sources and information about Ancient Civilizations and helped me with my research.

Special thanks to brave Amelia Earhart who flew the World and became a legend. This enormous effort and her achievements were made available to me in a full and detailed account of her life. It helped me in comparing my life, the life of an Ancient Maya Priest with her life and proved that the Spirit of each person on Earth has many lives. I am deeply grateful for the gift she passed onto me, as a newborn person, who now carries the same Spirit: her experience and knowledge in biology, medicine, art, writing, and drawing, which she acquired and developed during her lifetime. I am thankful for her enormous strength and love for life and adventure. All of this priceless Spirit development is deeply appreciated by all other re-born people in these Spirits and those who will be reborn in future and continue to carry Spirit light through the chain of lives.

Thanks to the Ancient Maya Priest who gave me wisdom, knowledge about the other side of life: energy, auras, how to connect with Spirits, Gods and Goddesses. All of which were passed onto me in the form of an amazing friendship with plants, animals and echoing rocks; understanding their tender souls. I am also grateful to him for passing onto me his enormous strength, love and care for his people. He helped them survive through terrible droughts in Mexico and he was strong enough to sacrifice his own son for their wellbeing.

To my lifelong friend and companion in my dreams, the Holy Spirit, my Guide who lives somewhere in the Universe, on the Other Side and for giving me support, helping me travel in my dreams through the planet and our Universe. He is the one who was talking to me

throughout the years, teaching me and educating me in my dreams and helping me connect with other Spirits, Gods and Goddesses. I give you prayerful thanks.
To some amazing High Power and to my extended family on the Other Side, who are my Guardian Angels, who care about me, and who help me navigate in this life to avoid danger, make the right decisions and warn me ahead of time by talking to me daily through the numbers' code, I give thanks.

Special thanks to GOD who blessed me and saved my life, and as a result, enabling me to write this book.

THE PRIEST

Strange and amazing things have happened in my life since I visited the Chichén Itza archeological site in Mexico in January, 2008. Before that day, I was a scientist, a business person with a mother's responsibility, just like millions of people around. My life changed forever after this visit.

The way I saw the world changed dramatically! The way people saw me also changed. The most amazing thing was that wild animals started to accept me as if I was part of their world and nature. Suddenly, I wanted and I started talking to them in the same way we talk between humans and they started listening to me, following me and even doing what I asked them to do. It surprised me and other people who became witnesses of this occurrence. In one sentence, I can describe it this way: Wisdom has come to me and touched my soul and I became wise.

Here is my story.

"Equinox! Equinox! Equinox!" I woke up and continued to say this strange word over and over again.

I see, in front of me, huge, beautiful, orange tulips inside a green vase with gold drawings on it. The morning sunlight is shimmering through the water in the vase . . . and I smell the sweet fragrance of spring.

The Priest

At the time, we lived near the mountains in Tibet and my father, every year, gave these tulips to my mother as a gift on her Birthday. He was a scientist, studying plants. He told me that these kinds of tulips grow very high in the mountains. Their name is *Greg's Tulips*.

My mother lifted me from my bed, took me into her arms and hugged me... I studied her face, her eyes. I knew she was worried, because I woke up again with the same dream, with this strange word in my mind and I didn't have any idea what it meant. I felt guilty, because I loved my mother and father so much that I didn't want them to worry because of me. My mother told me always that I was a very good child....

Suddenly, I remembered that I just saw a huge snake in my dream; a snake slithering through the street at the back of our house. It was maybe 5 to 8 houses long. I became all excited and wanted to escape from my mother's embrace. I needed to jump from her arms and run to the street to check if the snake was still there....

"Mommy, I need to run fast outside now. Please let me go, big snake there.... Let's go with me, I want to show it to you... It is a very nice big snake. She is kind and wise like an old king in the book you read to me. Today in my dream she talks to me with her soft voice.... Please Mommy, please let's go!"

It first started when I was two and half years old and my parents were really worried – they didn't know what this word Equinox meant. I grew up in the country where no one was using it and no one knew what it meant. No one spoke English there.

Julia – the Little Priest

I had hundreds of dreams during my life about pyramids and white, beautiful palaces, huge crystals, turquoise oceans with white sand beaches, animals, birds and fruits, which did not exist in my country and in our world. I also saw strange people with unusual outfits and drawings like tattoos on their faces and hands. I saw very big, tall people and I saw myself the same size as they were.

I saw ancient Gods, Goddesses, those always of extremely big sizes... Sometimes, I woke up and continued talking in another language; repeating again and again the same word, the meaning of which I didn't know.

Some of my dreams reoccurred – I saw them a few times, for example this one about a pyramid: In my dream, I am inside the temple, on the top of the pyramid. The pyramid is cut on top. Lots of people below are waiting for me to start something very important – some kind of ritual. Everything is ready. I see, on a tray, amazing orange see-through fruits and unusual ritual things. I sneak, kind of hiding, and try to look through the white curtains. Down below, I see people waiting. I am ready to start...and I woke up each time.

I grew up in Europe and I always knew that pyramids existed in Egypt, but they all had a pointed top. When I moved to Canada 17 years ago, my friend told me that she also saw some pyramids near Mexico City. I asked her if these pyramids were cut on top. She said, "NO, they're kind of round on top."
I continued to think that it was just one of my dreams, nothing more....

On January 2, 2008, I visited Mexico and Chichen Itza for the first time in my life. When I walked through the alley, where local people sell souvenirs, I instantly knew that I lived here before. My whole body was covered in goose-bumps! I recognized these white-barked trees and this special light going through the trees and the white soil.

When I saw the pyramid, I knew – I felt it instantly – this is it! Here I am. This is the pyramid I saw in my dreams so many times during my life. It was impossible to explain, but I felt a connection with the Maya people around me, the people who were selling souvenirs. I immediately felt an affinity toward them and I liked them a lot. This young boy tried to sell me some masks. A small-size, wrinkled grandmother walked toward me in the crowd. It just felt as if I had returned home, to my mother land, and I felt that these people around me were almost like my relatives! I bought some souvenirs just to make them happy and I enjoyed seeing the happy smile on this boy's face.

It was a very short visit in Chichen Itza that day, less than a few hours. Most of the time, I stayed with the group of tourists, gathering around our tour guide and listening to him. Waves of goose bumps continued to flow through my body during his talk. The problem was that I knew nothing – zero – about Mayan history, culture or architecture prior to this day. I bought this travel package shortly before my departure and there was no time to study anything. Now it all started to be really interesting. I tried to remain close to the guide and sometimes I asked questions.

At one point during the tour, the guide started describing the Maya leaders. He told us that they were wearing sandals, big bracelets on their legs and hands and big jewelry around the neck made from shells, jade and feathers, short cotton dress, sometimes with jaguar skin on top. Also he mentioned that there was a legend saying that a very long time ago; some man came here with blond hair and green eyes...

Suddenly, a German tourist pointed directly at me and said that the tour guide may have made a mistake because he was describing me. It was funny, but it was exactly what he described. I was wearing my favorite jaguar print jacket on top of a short cotton dress, sandals and big bracelets on my legs and hands made from shells and jade, and my hair is blond and I do have green eyes. When I was packing in Canada I felt that this outfit would be best in case I visited the pyramids in Mexico!

Deep inside, I was a little bit worried about this visit, because of all my previous dreams. For some reason, I wished to have my favorite outfit with me for support.... At the same time I felt like I was going to some kind of important celebration or party and I might meet someone I knew a long time ago. Two weeks later, I returned to Canada and told my friend that I saw the pyramid from my dream! She advised me to visit a hypnosis specialist, who was doing past life regression. As a scientist, I didn't believe that we have another life and that it would be possible to travel back to that time or even remember it. It sounded really silly to me, so I decided not to do this. Period. But this strange coincidence and feeling regarding the pyramid continued to invade my thoughts at every turn....

The next day I was sitting, as usual, on my favorite bench in Stanley Park, reading a magazine. One article attracted my attention. It was about a very famous doctor, Alfons Ven, from Holland. He discovered that our body has an invisible control system. This system controls the functions of our body, our metabolism and health. Most people are born healthy. During their lives people experience stress and as a result this control system goes "out of order", breaks down and can not control the body anymore. So the body starts to develop all kinds of illnesses. This amazing doctor prepares pills for his clients made of pure lactose. He uses them like a container for the important information he puts inside them to fix the control system, and to return it to normal. But not only this, Alfons also says: *"The intelligence of the preparations is so highly evolved that you are gently reconnected with your origin, with your authenticity, with the real you, your inner power."* WOW! This doctor is a genius!

There was a story in this article about a boy who had a big problem. He simply did not want to attend school. At all! Because his own father was working in that school and the boy did not feel comfortable; he was shy. Alfons asked him to do one thing while he prepared the treatment for this boy. He asked him to say aloud to the open window: "I am not more than somebody else, I am not less than somebody else, I am myself. And then you say your first name." It worked great with perfect result for this boy. As a scientist, all my life I have experimented with everything new. I looked around.... I was alone in this park. Only some Canadian wild geese were eating grass between rosebushes and cherry trees, and one big white-head eagle was sleeping on the pine tree across the rose garden. I repeated the magic words, aloud...! Suddenly, it struck me as a lightning from the sky directed to my origin. A miracle happened. I felt a heavenly, beautiful energy coming to me....

Doctor Alfons Ven is a real magical person living on Earth right now. GOD talks with people through him and sends this ray from heaven to each and everyone who is in touch with him! Just by reading this article I felt instantly – the very same day – that some amazing changes were beginning to take place. I organized my day like never before, full of energy and happiness. And this feeling of pure, fresh and dynamic energy is amazing!

I decided that day that I would visit my past life with the assistance of the hypnosis specialist and find out WHO I AM. Because when I tried to repeat this sentence at that moment, when I needed to say my name, my own name did not sound right! I needed to know WHO I AM! Soon after that, I am sitting in the chair in front of the famous hypnosis specialist, Diana Cherry. This woman is 80 years old with 60 years experience.

****

I came for the appointment 15 minutes early. It was a cute house with a sign on the door saying that her office was at the back of the house. I went there and decided to wait. I looked around. It was early spring and many plants around the backyard and patio were still dry and grey. It gave me the feeling that maybe no one lived here for a very long time.

A black cat arrived softly to the step ladder, sat near me and looked into my eyes; he sat for a while and then left. A squirrel ran to the patio and I noticed that there were lots of nuts on the ground waiting for it. It was silent and very peaceful in this backyard. Suddenly, out of nowhere a lot of black crows started landing on the neighbor's huge pine tree. They were cawing and screeching and it created such a big loud noise that I put my hands to my ears to avoid the deafening sound. There were way too many of them, maybe hundreds. I never saw so many all at once. At 10 a.m. precisely, I knocked on the door....

A woman with silver hair and turquoise, aquamarine eyes opened the door. She was wearing an aquamarine top – the same color as her eyes – it was a beautiful harmony! Smiling, she said, "Welcome, I am Di Cherry." She invited me to sit in front of her in a big comfortable chair. She gently put my legs up on a stool with a big pillow and covered them with some very brightly knitted blanket called an "afghan" to keep them warm. And we started. Di Cherry told me to relax and we went step by step through this process into a deeper and deeper relaxation level.... My feet and hands felt very heavy . . . my eyes were closed.

Reading #1, 13th of February 2008.

It felt as if Di's voice came through water to me.

(Note: The text below is a literal transcription of the first session –no editing.)

She began....

In your dream, you are in the temple on the top of the pyramid ready to start some ritual. You look down below; there are many people waiting for you to start.... What do you see around you?

I see instantly big huge eagle head near me!!! With bright yellow orange beak! WOW! A man is wearing a cape, made from many feathers; he wears sandals, bracelets, on the legs and hands, short skirt.... Another one across of me wearing long, kind of trench coat down to the floor, made like a snakeskin. It is a very well done coat, looks really neat and beautiful! It is made from dark grey colored polished scales, one to one. I see him from the back at that moment. He turns and looks directly at me very serious. He has high cheekbones, long slim eyes and he is tall, handsome man in his 40's. He has long spears in his hand... He is magnificent.

I see man staying near him with square-shaped hat, same shape as Nefertiti from Egypt had. Another man with mask like a fox or coyote....[1] *All these men wearing masks and an enormous amount of very big size jewels made from stones, rocks. Looks very beautiful and luxurious.... I look down and I see my muscular legs with toned skin and, like everyone else around, I wear short skirt and sandals. And I wear coat made from soft jaguar skin sides down to the floor and I feel this softness and see it from both sides.... To my big surprise I see them all wearing round big earrings! It is strange and funny. I never saw before men wearing earrings that look like big white buttons! I start laughing. I am sure that this part was a creation of my mind!* (I was sure about it... until I visited Chichen Itza for the second time and saw

---

[1] I saw another man with a mask like a fox or a coyote. After I visited Egypt, I have no doubt that this is an Anubis mask. I recognized it instantly when I saw it in Egypt. This Goddess is responsible for the mummification and protection of the dead on the Other Side.

pictures of men everywhere on the walls, who were all wearing this kind of round button earrings!)

Where were you an hour before?

I am inside in some building with white carved walls. In front of me, there was a very big book with jaguar skin cover.

What kind of book? Touch the page...

It is heavy, it is yellow color pages, and it is opening wide, like accordion folder paper. I saw two guard people staying near the open door . . . with long spears in their hands.

Why do you read this book?

An incredibly strong feeling come over me... my voice suddenly changed... and now it was full of emotions. Suddenly, I was drawn deeply into these emotions....
It is such a hard responsibility for me! .....I need to make the right decision today...right decision. I am the one who make decisions...my people are waiting. And I saw the page and their round Maya calendar and I studied it.... It is very hard to make decision today...big responsibility to make announcement when to start to plant seed to the ground...rain needs to be short after...I need to know when rain season will start...we have a drought.

Suddenly, I started talking much louder, almost screaming: *"WATER! WATER!!! People need water to have harvest! They need harvest! They work so hard.... Their life so difficult...."* Streams of tears started running down my face; my tears were two rivers of tears... I never had such tears in my whole life! The muscles on my face, which I never used before, made a sorrow mask... I feel an ENORMOUS spirit PAIN come out. I was talking in a different voice and used different muscles on my face!

It was overwhelming and I didn't have any control over what was going on. I never experienced something like this in my entire life...

At this point I am the Highest Priest in this pyramid and I am full of emotions and feeling....

"Let's back up to the pyramid," Di Cherry's voice told me.
What is the reason for this gathering?

I see round shape, it come again and again in my vision... now I see it. It is a ball.

You're up there and people are waiting...

I see three stone tables and I saw a light coming from an entrance on the opposite side. I stay on the left side...
On one of the tables, I see a man lying down...
He is the winner today! He is very proud!! And happy. And he is ready to die now to help people... and to be sacrificed... and I continue crying and talking with great emotion. *These people will give everything what they have to GOD, most best what they have... best of their people... in order to have harvest.*

Come close, look into their eyes. People can change gender, the color of their hair or skin, their whole looks, BUT if you look into their eyes, you will recognize who the person is. Maybe it is someone you know from this life.

The Priest

I step closer... I am afraid to look into his eyes...tears run down my face and suddenly a loud scream come out from my throat....

Di Cherry stopped the session. She decided that this was excessively emotional for me.

The last question she asked was:
Let's go to the end of your life there, your last year, where are you, what do you see?

I see big huge grey snake made of stone....

****

It was a very strange feeling to see, to look at people around me on the street right after my past life readings.... They were all so preoccupied with this present life! Some of these people were in such a crazy rush to get to their cars. Some of them were way too emotional, intense, even angry..., fighting on the phone even on the street. Some of them looked sad....

At that time, my business partners were grieving because we lost a very special old friend.... He was a wise, 80-year-old, an Honorable Supreme Buddhist Monk. It was very sad. I wished for my partners to know that first, he is in a much better place than we have here on Earth, and that he will be re-born – if he decides to do so. Secondly, they will meet this person again in heaven after they die themselves, while waiting there to start living their next lives. There is also a possibility that they will meet him again during their future lives. I was hoping that this knowledge would support them and all other people who lost a loved one. Because now, I know for sure that people have many lives.

I wish that all of these people on the street could have the possibility to see themselves for a moment from the side of the road where one life follows another and another. Such possibility can give them a new way of evaluating their present life and enjoy it much more. It is very important for them to know that, YES; they have this life in this body. BUT when they die, the Spirit they have inside them will not die! Never! It just does not work that way. Spirits cannot die! Spirits will continue to exist in a new body in the next life, period. Now that I know this, I am guarantying it for each and everyone. Spirit's life will go on and continue to live in many future lives. Those special skills a person is developing now will be useful in his/her next life. It is important for everyone to visit a past life regression specialist at least once to make adjustments for their development.

Who was I before? What kind of skills did I have? Our problems in this life can have roots in our past lives. Most people just don't know this and are suffering not in one life, but maybe throughout a chain of lives by carrying this emotional baggage with them from one life to the next. The only way to fix it, to get rid of this burden, is to visit a past life regression specialist. We all have a doctor for the body; I am glad that doctors for the Spirit exist as well.

I really wish to say to all of these people on the street that we have many lives and that the life we have now is really easy to live, not that bad at all! Enjoy your life! Make people around you happy in your presence...! Skip fighting with your close friends, with the people you love.... These problems, which you are facing today, right now, and which look BIG to you, are really NOTHING when compared to the problems people had a long time ago during their lives in ancient Mexico. You have food and water and you will have water tomorrow and after tomorrow and for a long, long time. You are very lucky that you don't know what the word DROUGHT really means.... I wish to tell people: WATER is the most important part of people's lives. Please, each and everyone, take care of your WATER now and of the future water supply. Do what you can to be sure it is safe, clean and will be always available to everyone who needs it on our planet.

****

When I left Di Cherry's place and I look back one more time at this cute house, I had a different view of this place, compared to how I saw it before. Now I see this house as a secret Star Gate to the past – to the ancient world, thousands of years ago. And this smiling, innocent, angelic-looking Di Cherry, in reality, is a wise, magic person; she is making such magic for everyone who consults her.

I never had entertainment like this! This is the best possible quality entertainment on Earth! You can be inside of your life, back thousands of years ago and you can see everything in color, you can touch things around you and you are part of your real past life!

I had arrived that day at Di Cherry's place alone. When I left her house, there were two people inside me.... It was an astonishing feeling – me and my self as a Priest, altogether as one person.

When I returned home that day and looked in the mirror I could not recognize my own face! After a few hours of exercise during the past life session this muscle, which I never use before, created a new "mask" on my face. This "Stamp" from my past was there for 3 or 4 days, and even now, people see a shadow of it and tell me that something changed in my face!

After the first two hypnosis sessions, I was staying again at the same hotel in Rivera Maya, Mexico. It was just 2.5 months later. The people who worked there and remembered me from my first visit told me that my face had changed somehow and that it looked different. I guess I just started to be older – by 2000 years.

The Priest was a guest in my mind during the next 2 or 3 weeks after the hypnosis sessions. From time to time, during the day, I had visions and feelings. During the night, in my dreams, I saw myself in Chichen Itza carrying on with my daily routine. I enjoyed the Priest's presence and continued to remember more and more of my life as a High Priest in ancient Mexico.

I remembered my two hairdressers, who worked my hair into such an unusual hairstyle every day. They lifted up my black, long, thick hair and attached all this heavy jewelry and feathers to it. It was similar to the hairstyle that Japanese women have on ancient pictures.

Once, I started remembering that I had received a very special gift from the far north city. It was a little baby jaguar, which was white – a very rare color! He was born with twisted, bended toes in his front right paw. It was impossible to fix. He was small and never grew to its full size. This baby followed me everywhere and slept nearby. I guess he accepted me as his mother because I always wore a jaguar cape. He had green, jade jewelry on the collar around his neck. I loved him and gave him the name of "White star". The word *Zolkin* or *Zolkan* came often to my mind after I woke up those days and I didn't know what it meant.[2] I remember that I had a

[2] I did not know what *Zolkin* meant in Mayan, until December 2008 when I found the same word in a book, but with a T in front! It was name for the Mayan Calendar! *The tzolk'in, the most fundamental and widely-attested of all the Maya calendars, was a*

live turtle as a pet as well. This turtle lived with the previous Priest and we had it in the temple for many years. The turtle had a round, tattoo-like mandolin drawing on her carapace. I brought this turtle to the observatory *Caracol*, because the jaguar had begun hunting it and had tried to bite her. I remember living in the white carved building, now named the Annex to the Nunnery. Near the entrance, on the wall, there is a bas relief of me as a Priest with luxuriant hair including two pony tails.

I often walked in the dark to the observatory after a sauna, and enjoyed staring to the night sky, studying the stars. I love studying sounds as well. Very much! I even wrote a manuscript about the sounds of the rocks. Once, I found a stone – it was my favorite limestone – a big flat, white, grey rock. I found it deep in the cave and it produced a beautiful sound. I tried pounding this rock with different size shells and other pebbles and it made beautiful sounds – like many bells made of glass or crystals. This often put me in a trance somehow.

****

The mystery around the sounds echoing from the Chichen Itza pyramid is still not solved.[3] Dr. Steven J. Waller has proposed that prehistoric rock art, which is usually found in echoing locations such as caves and canyons, was produced in response to the echoes, since legends from many ancient cultures describe the belief that echoes were spirit voices. *"Where else in the history*

---

pre-eminent component in the society and rituals of the ancient Maya. The word, meaning "count of days", was coined based on Yukatek Maya. From Wikipedia, the free encyclopedia

[3] The Priest loved to study sounds; maybe he was the one who knew the secrets of the sounds produced in the pyramid of Chichen Itza.

of the world have an ancient people preserved a sacred sound by coding it into stone so that a thousand years later people might hear and wonder," (An archaeological study of chirped echo from the Mayan pyramid of Kukulcan at Chichen Itza by David Lubman.

It is Interesting that every spring, for many years, I bought the smallest size turtle for my sister, Elena's birthday on April 10. In the fall, we would return the turtle back to nature. The place where I bought the turtles belonged to a company, which caught wild animals to send them all over the world to different Zoos. There were snow-jaguars among the lot. They looked exactly like regular jaguars and belong to the same family, but their fur is white and their eyes are icy blue. Their local name is *Irbis*. The Latin name is *Uncia* (Shreber, 1775). They are very rare and part of the "RED book" of protected species. They live in Tibet, Altai, in Central Asia. During my early school years, I visited that place and stared at the white jaguars for many hours. That species is the largest among the panther's family and they are very powerful. Sometimes it was very scary to be right near the cage, when they jumped or roared. I was very lucky that the director let me go into the company's territory, because he knew my father very well. It was also interesting that the workers at that place brought back lots of turtles from the desert and kept them as live-meat to feed the snow jaguars. They even had a special machine, which crushed their shells. I had totally forgotten about this – it was many years ago! It was only yesterday, when I talked to my father, that he reminded me about it! Wow! Now I found a reason for having such an attraction to the jaguars – I had my own little, white jaguar in my past life as a Priest! This is what attracted me as a magnet near the cages of these huge, scary, white cats.

A young white jaguar

Reading #2 & 3 - 20th of February and 25th of March 2008

You can hear this reading, as well as Reading # 4, April 29, 2008, on the CD, which can be purchased at www.ameliareborn.com.

Reading # 2

(Note: This literal transcription from the recorded reading – no editing)

Cherry:

We are leaving this room, to eternity...through the centuries back... Back to the land we called Mexico. Sunshine.... Long time ago, and in your dream you're in the temple? You remember the temple? Do you? Not? You remember standing there? It is a day like so many, of sun and a clear blue sky. No thunder, no rain...a clear blue sky... smell the heat. You're so busy; so many things to do.... So much needs to be done. Hurrying here, hurrying there...people to direct, meals must be attended...and you know someone else prepares them. This is the day when you are in the temple, way on top of the pyramid. You are ready to start some ritual and look down below, lots of people waiting for you to start. Are you able to see those people now?

(I start talking with a voice that sounded strange even to me....)

I see this room, on top it is very cool, cool walls, it is cold walls upstairs. But it's crazy hot, very, very hot outside and so dry land, like powder land and all trees around dry...very, very dry, and its very hot...it sunshine killing.... Yes so many people and they waiting and it is very hot for them to wait and I need to start soon. Yes I am in cool place upstairs, it is cold walls and it is nice....

Are you up already or are you ascending those steps?

You know I am still there...I am still there....

Where are you at this time?

I see myself; I can run to this pyramid very fast! And when you ask if I am up or down I see myself one morning, I am running up to this so fast, like almost flying. I know each of these steps, I remember each of these steps and I am not afraid to run fast, fast, fast down.

YES.
I see it and I am enjoying actually run through this pyramid up and down...

So you have a speech or duty today, something important to do...Do you feel you're governing, you are ruling, you are a Priestess, a Priest?

(Suddenly, my voice changes)
I am a Priest, I am a Priest in this pyramid and it is such a big responsibility to be Priest, it is hard, so hard, impossibly hard! It is my people, so many people, they waiting for me, it is my people...I care about this people.... It is big responsibility; it is hard to be Priest.... They waiting for me, it is so dry, they don't have food, we need rain season. We need rain! We need rain, we need water, and we need water so hard, it is so dry... It is so dry around. We need WATER.

I understand.

They need to know when to start planting seeds, they need to know this. And I need to know and I can not make mistake. We need to put seed right before rain season. We need water... when we put seed to the ground. We need water very hard. We need water, water most important. We need rain. We need to pray to have rain. People waiting...they ready give everything what they have, best what they have... to have water. They need water....

Right.

We have droughts.... We have droughts, we need water, people will need water, and people will give anything for the water. And this day is so important, we pray God to help us and we need to make sacrifice..... We need to give; gift to the God.

And what is to be the gift today?

It is so hard... it so hard.... (My voice is very, very sad.) *We have game today, we have big game today.*

YES.

We choose best people to play in this game; best people we have to play in this game...and we have winner, we already have winner. It is all about ball, it is beautiful blue ball and this is the winner of the ball.

It is a rubber ball is it?

Yes, it is rubber ball and it is dark blue color...it little bit color broke some place... they put on top this color, but it is blue color.... Yes, it is very important day....

And the winner, you're going to take him up to the pyramid? Is he going to be on the top of the pyramid?

Yes, he's so proud today, he so happy. He's so proud, he win the game, he's so proud today...But he going to die...he going to die!

But, he knows this, doesn't he?

Yea...Everybody knows this! Everybody knows this and this is so hard...

This is the way of the people honoring the God ... he is going to give himself – great honor for himself...

YES... (Crying)

The Priest

Being fine young men...and so...this sacrifice needs to be done in this room or above?

In this room. He went up, they bring him up and he has garlands of flowers, he has flowers...it is droughts.... People find flowers and they make for him...flowers...they washed him...like a shower... and put on him all kind of oils, they have nice smell oils, he all with this like perfume things.... He's very beautiful, he have short skirt, and very tone muscles...and sandals, he has sandals...and necklaces and bracelets and on the legs he have bracelets and it is very rich and beautiful...very beautiful. It is so much stones, very beautiful many stones, I guess it is very expensive, very beautiful outfit he has....

I like you to look to this young man for a moment. Does he have dark blue eyes like you?

YES, he has blue eyes like me...[4] (Pause)

It is very hard day, it so hard day for me... it was hard day for me....difficult day for me....

But this is the great honor?

O....No! ... No... no.... (I start screaming, crying and talking through the crying.)
This is my son...this is the son, my son...the only one son I have... (I start crying hard.)

I am going to take you back before this day, I am going to take you to time when you were with your son and you were happy.

---

4 During another reading we found that the Priest had dark blue eyes...

...I am fine...we still up...I need to do my job now...I need to do my job now...
He is on the table, he on the right side, I turn him to the right side.... I have in front of me men with Eagles mask, big Eagle mask and this mask.... Eagle has yellow mouth, orange yellow mouth...I saw another man, he has long coat and he has slim eyes, very slim eyes and high cheek. And he look at me right now, he looks at me; because now most important moment...and we look to each other...we talk with our eyes....

He has long coat and this coat is made from huge snake or like a snake...with many, many scales, beautiful! The scales are side by side. And he has a long stick on the top sharp, with black sharp end. And many feathers and skins of all kinds of animals around...And I have a long coat and this one is made from Jaguar, it's a jaguar coat.... I have Jaguar coat and now.., and now most important moment... (Voice trembles)

...I say bye to my son and I kiss him and I touch him and say to him bye and this is so stressful.... (Crying) *And now he on his side.... and now...*

And now...

I give him some kind of plants juice to drink, something makes him sleep and he just sleeps. And it's made from kind of mushrooms and kind of bulbs from the flowers and roots all together and he sleeps now....
(My voice start to be strong and solid)

But his Spirit aware, his spirit aware and ready.... And ready to start....

Right.

The Priest

We pray and we make some rituals...some kind rituals, kind of strange things people doing...and they brings cups and they already have cups around, I don't want see these cups...they have this white cups for the blood...to collect blood....

That's right.

I need to make this Spirit FREE; I need to talk with his spirit now. It is very important to be very organized and cold minded to make it right. He is the winner...from all people who was in this game. They all try; each of them tries the best to win.... Each of them tries hard to win, very hard to win.

They all try to concentrate on this ring. They try to concentrate as much as they can...and I see level of the concentration of energy. I see this energy near each person who plays, I see their energy and I see color of energy also. I see blue color and orange color and kind of red color...and they are all playing and I am sitting and all my people and EAGLE and SNAKE and all other guards and warriors and we look. My people see the color, we see color of concentration, and we know: those who win have today most strong highest level of concentration of energy. And we need someone, we need MESSENGER to the GOD, we need those who will reach GOD ears.

YES.

Symbol of the BALL is the message to put to GOD ears, and we need someone who best with this today. Yes, he sleep, his spirit strong, his spirit ready to bring the message to GOD, he is waiting now for action. I see his body now with many layers...many layers, you can see them through, but it's one, two, tree, four, five six, seven, maybe eight...layers of his body and up and up, one by one, kind of his body also and ...one of those more round...round. This one I need to start with, this one most important....and now ...all my concentration going to him. I need to take out from his body his spirit, his Spirit Body.

YES.

Now. And, and it is heavy work.... My hands start to be so heavy...very heavy...my hand near his back and I'm opening it and I take out from inside this round sphere and I try to take it out and it is very difficult and going out very slow...very slow...it's going out. It's kind of light when it's inside...but when it's coming out, it starts so stuffy, heavy, like a honey, strong. And I take out and I make effort and I make it like with help of strongest vacuum. Out, take it out this thing and now it's in the air right near me...it comes out finally all. It's a flat, big huge gong or disk, like a gong. Chinese people have gong like this and they make sound with this...this things now very heavy and it make sound.... Hmmmmm ... wuuuuuuu ... heavy, down sound ... very down deep sound. I put it in big container for now, like a vase, like a vase...until I will deliver it to GOD.

YES.

And all people, all my people around already closed their noses and ears to avoid that spirit goes in to their body.

Interesting!

So it's closed now, they breathe through their mouths very little. Spirit runs to anyone's body around trying to find new body.[5]

---

[5] Spirits can run to anyone's body trying to find a new body. Explanation: we have an Astral body, our EFIR body. In this case, the astral body, will go to God with a message, while, at

YES.

And this is more than a live thing now, so all closed their noses and their ears. Guards, these warriors they're waiting and they have the same... (Pause)

This part, I don't want to talk... (Sad voice) *I see blood; I see they collect blood from his neck to these white containers, to this big bowl.... I see this...* (Pause)
They're giving me his heart.... I have his heart, in my left hand his heart and I have ball in my right hand and I am going down to people and I show them the heart and ball.

This is Heart of the Winner...
This is heart of my son... (Crying)

All these people below have little containers. Little white cups, round cups. And to each cup only one drop of his blood coming, each cup one drop, only one drop. They will bring this cup to their homes, to their plants, to their fields. They will mix with water and they will put this Holy Water to the plants to have harvest, to have plants to grow.

This Sacrifice Blood, Holy Blood will turn to Plants and Flowers and Fruits... and give them LIFE to live....

---

the same time, there is a possibility that during this process, our EFIR or the ephemeral body, without the energy support from the astral body will try to find a new owner, another body.

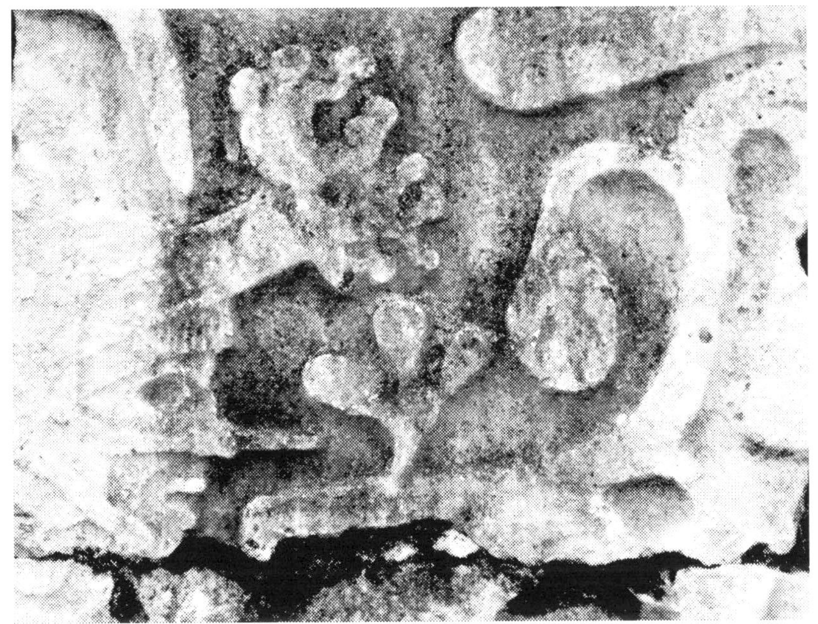

Details of the bas-relief from the wall in Ball court in Chichen Itza

The warriors have their noses closed to avoid the spirit going inside their bodies. They are near plants, the symbol of harvest, growing from bulbs into fruits from the sacrificed blood.

Right.
(Long pause)

Are you willing to go back to his childhood?

No.... it is very emotional, I don't want to talk about him anymore.

Can I ask you who teaches you to do these rituals?

I will tell now. I am Priest in this temple, in this big beautiful temple. My responsibility is to take care of the plants and harvest and agriculture. And astrology. I have many students, I have people who only study planets and they study in Caracol, our observatory. This is my responsibility. Sometimes, I bless little children, very little children, newborn children. And I like to heal little children and I just heal yesterday an old, very old and sick and slim old man and I remember him. Sometimes I am a doctor and I have KNOWLEDGE. My knowledge comes from far...far away time...my knowledge split between maybe 10 people, they're carrying this part through their lifetime and if I am dead, they all come to one, new Priest, and they each give their part. I am the only one who knows everything about this; my responsibilities. This is my subjects, deep...very deep. I have a book, I have a big old book, it comes from previous Priest and it is a heavy book. I can hardly lift this book, it's so heavy. Many numbers in this book and I see calendar.... I see this big calendar; this is astrological round calendar, the size of the whole page and many calculations, math and some drawings, and letters....

The first few days after this session were very hard. I tried to avoid my thoughts about this sacrifice. Emotions and tears kept invading my mind. I tried to avoid people. Imagine if someone would ask me why I was crying – how could I answer? "O...yesterday I sacrificed my son, because we had droughts...." What would people think? Imagine the expression on their faces? They would think I had gone completely out of my mind.

A few months later, I found this description of the game I visualized during my life-regression session. Di Cherry and I were surprised to read this. It supports everything I saw!

The more ancient type of sacrifice in Maya – is an idea of sending a messenger to the deity in the name of the whole community. The soul of the sacrificed person after his death was freed from the body and went to gods and delivered requests and prayers of people. The human sacrifice by no means represented any kind of "exceptional brutality". This act was perceived as sending of the selected, best of the best person to gods – similar to Jesus Christ the Savior. Indians were constantly surprised by brutality of the inhabitants of the Old World, who crucified Jesus without any special drug thus causing his unbearable physical suffering. Indians perceived Him as a messenger to the Only God. More than that, in ancient times, messengers to gods were sent only in exceptional or difficult situations. Messengers were supposed to solicit for wellbeing and prevention of disasters. Messengers to gods were either regular (in particular feasts) or in exceptional cases, like: crop failure, drought, epidemics, etc. ("Ancient America: Flight in time and prostransive. Mezoamerika" Excerpts from the book by GG Ershovoy UnCopyrighted©Sam, 2003-2006)

The complication derived from the dividing and uniting space between the world of living and the world of dead ones. It was usually depicted as quite realistic image of the upper layer of earth with a crack, where, on one hand, the soul of the dead falls down, and from where the sprout of new life emerges. Sometimes it was depicted in a form of open jaws – of a jaguar, reptile, or bird. However, the soul of a person in order to transcend this space should separate itself from the body. Naturally, it was happening most often after the death of the body. But sometimes the soul could leave the body in a time of sleep or sickness. And in very particular moments the selected magicians were able to do it – priests and naguali – by using special practices and devices, for example, taking psychedelic substances. As a rule, for transcendence of this dangerous space the special connectives were needed. The mountain lord of the darkness – jaguar was the chief purifier of souls in the underworld. ("Ancient America: Flight in time and prostransive. Mezoamerika" Excerpts from the book by GG Ershovoy UnCopyrighted©Sam, 2003-2006)

A few months later, after the first hypnosis readings with Di Cherry, I was walking through the Duty Free stores at the international airport. Suddenly, I saw something which took my breath away – literally – I stopped breathing. I saw through the store window some jacket with the exact snake skin coat, which I saw during my hypnosis session! It was an astonishing feeling! It was a Zilli store for luxury men's clothes and shoes. I went inside and ask the clerk to show me the jacket. It was made from real python skin!

Remember what I described during my first past life regression; suddenly I was in ancient Chichen Itza in the pyramid 2000 years ago....

Here is part of the description:

Another one across from me was wearing a long, kind of trench coat down to the floor, made of a snakeskin. It is a very well done coat, looks really neat and beautiful! It was made from dark grey color polished scales . . . I saw him from the back at that moment.

Now I know for sure that in my hypnosis session I saw an ancient Maya man who was wearing a cape from real snakeskin. It looked very similar to this one in the Zilli store![6] – with only two differences; the scales on the coat were smaller than those on the cape I saw in the ancient Chichen Itza temple. And 2000 years ago, there were no seams on the garment. It gave me the idea that, at that time, the snakes which existed then were much bigger than the pythons are today!

---

[6] www.zilli.fr

I wish I could have bought the jacket for me – it looked so beautiful! But it was available only for men. Wow! How lucky they are, they can feel themselves almost as a Kukulcan, the Serpent Snake God of Maya in this amazing Zilli jacket!

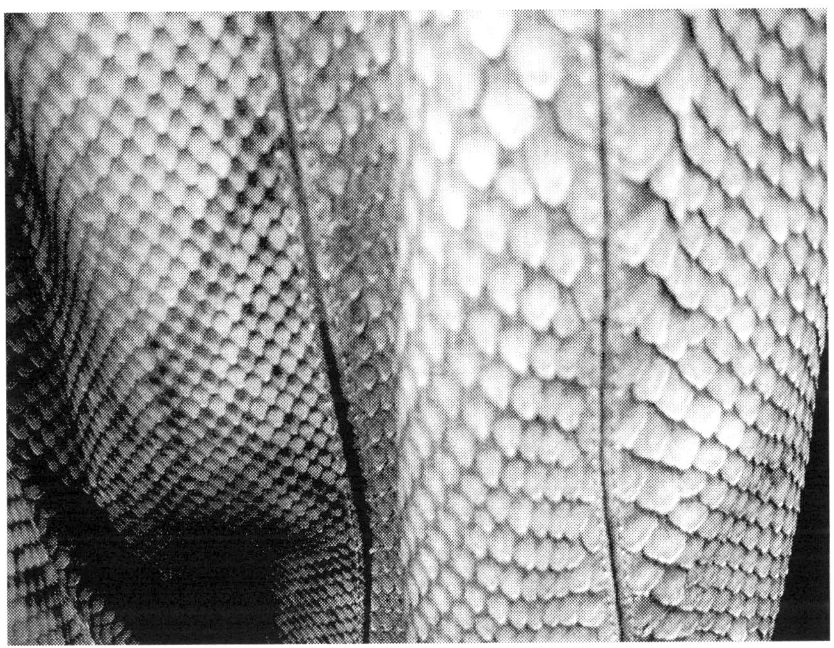

Snakeskin jacket

Below are dreams which I had at different times of my life. I didn't have any idea before, WHY I had these unusual dreams and I don't want to interpret them. I am not a specialist in the field. I just decided to add them here, because I know now that, in these dreams, there is an echo from my past lives. They also support what I saw and felt during my hypnosis sessions. They add some information and interesting details.

These dreams are exactly – word for word – how I told them after I woke up.[7]

In the dream below, for example, I experienced the process by which the SPIRIT BODY was taken out from my physical body.

Dream # 1
They pulled my body out of me, April 25, 1996

After a long time of suffering I dozed off at 6 am. It went on for many days. I could not have enough sleep. I asked to be helped falling asleep. It had been happening many times that my body turned off, became heavy as lead, dull, but my mind went on thinking. After that, a strange thing happened – it seemed that, I began falling asleep very deeply, as if falling into some pit, but the mind was not sleeping yet and partly in control. It happened immediately. It was horrible. I was lying there – inert. My entire body was heavy, I didn't feel it and suddenly some force began sucking me out of my body, pulling out like a pump, sucking milk out of the breast, forcefully, pulling out something out of me . . . but the shell of my body stayed there. They were pulling out my soul. It was a purely physical sensation and I observed it with my brain. At the same time, I was feeling how it was being pulled out of my self. All the while, I was still feeling my physical body. At the beginning I thought that it was simply a huge suction cup pulling my body up, but then, I noticed, that my body rested in its place....

---

[7] Please drop me a comment if you have an interpretation for my dreams or parts of them, if you know the meaning of the words or symbols. It will be very interesting to meet scientists who study Chichen Itza. I wish that they would ask me questions about the mystery that still surrounds the place. Perhaps I will be able to answer them – if these questions cover the time I lived in Chichen Itza.

I remembered how it was! I was lying on my right side, and everything was coming out from here, it is like when the sky is covered with clouds, and then an opening appears – it was in the middle of my back, over the waistline, closer to the left side, in the heart area. They were pulling slowly and with great force – the spirit body was coming out of the skin with difficulty. There was a moment, when this thing almost came out, but had not separated completely; a laden, heavy thing was hanging over me. It may have not been heavy, but it was pulled out with such difficulty, tightly – that is why I felt this laden heaviness. It was like a sphere, like a shape of the spiral galaxy, the thing being pulled out, larger than a meter. It was hanging over my body. My mind was on its own, I was looking from the inside and from the outside at the same time. Then I experienced some sensations, which I can neither describe, nor tell about. I felt with my eyes some rounded protruding surface, some drops of temperature, then I crashed out totally and didn't remember anything afterwards. Maybe the body in the dream was dead after this "experiment"...?

Dream # 2
Hieroglyphs on the palm, September 12, 1992

I was sitting on the hill, the hill of yellow clay, leaning my back against the hill. There were similar hillocks around, the size of about two meters, not more. Some oval form. I realized that I looked at my palm, the left one. There was a drawing on the palm – a sign almost as big as the palm. As if it was stamped by a stamp of a very good quality. There were no chiromancy lines on the palm. There was a white rim, like a closed circle. And some colors. Such colors are painted on cakes – meringue – rosy, protuberant and dried on. And it was like that; each line very clear and they stuck out over the skin.[8] Apart from white, there also was red, and, maybe also brown-beige and black. It was a three-dimensional, complicated figure. The lines did not merge, as if they were drawn under a microscope. It looked very much like a hieroglyph, but a hieroglyph is always based on a square frame – this one was rounded. At least one side was curved.

I was looking for a long time, and then I saw two women approach me, native Indians, wearing clothes of a fabric with streaming, iridescent pattern. I recognized them. I said, "Oh, I haven't seen you for a long time." I said, "Look, I have a sign," and stretched out my hand to them. They started looking. (I remembered all this with difficulty, as if through thick honey, or layers of water; every word was hard to utter.) They also said about me: "You are a Goddess, and there is also one more person."

I asked them, "Where are you, where are you coming from, what is your life like?"

They said, "We can show you," and laughed with a rustling sound. "You probably should know yourself."

They said, "Because you have capabilities, energy," (specific energy in dreams).

I know I am used to make a plan, and remember everything in my dreams. I break everything in my dreams into parts, fragments. And I have a capacity of automatically storing in my memory major moments, coordinates. However, since I was 16 then, I always threw out of my memory all the unnecessary information and I controlled my thoughts. They knew

[8] The Maya word Tlappalan means land of red and black. Black, red, brown-beige are the colors the Maya usually used for their tattoos. All tattoos on the face are flat drawing, but they are as if embossed over the skin surface.

this. And they told me, that if I wanted to, I could keep all of my dreams in my memory. And I could wake up, coming back to them years and years later.

They said, "You will see and remember all of the details, every hour." (And this will enable me to change the past and the future – if I would go to them often then I would see and remember the future more clearly.)

They also said that people cannot remember this even if they get there. And this would make no sense to them, and they would not get their experience there. From that comment, I thought that maybe people do not have enough energy. If I knew which step brought me to what, then it would become possible for me to plan my own life and change my life.

Dream # 3
ATHARVAN, October 13, 1989

In the morning, I remembered the word from yesterday – EQUINOX, I was repeating it yesterday all the time. It was there before my waking up, always like a drop of water pecking the stone. EQUINOX... EQUINOX... EQUINOX....
Now I have the same sensation. But this time the word is different. This was like a flow, repeating the same word.... It was only one minute. I woke up, looked toward the window and closed my eyes again. And at this moment (I felt a shiver on my skin); I immediately saw the face of a man of a huge size. Maybe it was an enormous statue. My field of view captured an eye, a cheek, the chin on the left side. I was so staggered, shaken, that it disappeared. Afterwards, it appeared again, and again – I am stunned – it disappeared.

It was the face of a man, made of grey marble. But there was a feeling that he was alive. On the side there was a

pattern, something I saw on Chinese walls in China, and on his face there were many, many manuscripts of a very fine design. The face was of a single-color, and the pattern on the edge of the chin – a darker shade. The curvy writing was on the cheek in a triangle shape. He had Persian, almond-shaped eyes. And there was a word, which stuck with me, much harder than the word EQUINOX – it was repeating again and again ... constantly, rapidly. In my dream I thought that I would forget it, when I woke up. So I tried to remember. Maybe two words – avatar. And the word "vat" or "tar". I composed it from three words "vat", "tara". Something that was repeating all the time – "avatar", and somewhere there was also the word, "hat".
A V A T A R A ... A H A T A V A R A ...- Atharvan, maybe?

Yes! Exactly that word! I think it was the word. It was this one, whose face I saw. But I could not bear it, only for a moment, then everything blurred, I could not bear to look for a long time. I was there for an instant – a few times. Just like a quantum of light[9] of grey-dim color. It was not a marble – marble shine. I could draw it, how it was, what proportions there were. The finest drawing, as if his face was the size of a room, but traced with exquisite precision. (I drew this picture immediately after I woke up. I never expected that it would be featured in a future book.) Was he sleeping? I don't remember. He radiated the sensation of a living being. And I did not feel that I was sleeping.

---

[9] You will find Scientific Interpretation about quantum light at the end of the book, "The Re-birth of an Atlantean Queen" by Julia SvadiHatra.

Atharvan

Atharvan (अथर्वन् *, atharvan-; an n-stem with nominative singular* अथर्वा *atharvā)*
Vedic atharvan is cognate with Avestan *atharvan, "priest", but the etymology of the term is not yet conclusively established. (Boyce, 1982:16)*

Dream # 4
Baby from the river, April 11, 1992

High up in the mountains there was a giant castle, the Palace. Inside, there was a ball. I was the principal queen there. Some noble mothers brought their newborn babies there. It was some kind of tradition; they would bring their babies, and the ball is in honor of that. They are either initiated, or it is some sort of a ritual. The babies are nice, beautiful. They all are my people, and I have a right to do anything with anybody. I could keep any of their babies as a tribute.

I went outside, unnoticed. It was grey dawn and I saw a deep, deep canyon with a river running down at the bottom. The river was flowing out of the mountain; you could hear the sound of running water. And I found a baby there. He was lying in something like a nutshell – comfortable, in a good sleeping berth lined with silk and jewels. He seemed not to be dressed at all, but decorated all over! His body was entirely covered with something that resembled hieroglyphs, probably painted. His face, as if Mexican – eyes like olives, the nose as if Indian. There were similar wavy lines on his lips and nose. He had an unusual face with dark blue eyes. I brought him into the Palace, to keep him. They all surrounded me, surprised.

****

Maybe it was the priest who found the baby with dark blue eyes – I wonder.
As you noticed in the last three dreams the tattoo subject is repeated. There are tattoos on the palm of the hand, on the face and on the entire body of the baby. I asked myself why I had these dreams many times in my life. I never had any interest in visiting any tattoo parlor. However, now I know; I was simply a Maya Priest a few thousand years ago.

****

Here is the amazing story of a Miracle Man living in our time in Brazil. What I saw during my hypnosis sessions and in my dreams – how the Spirit Body leaves our physical body – is the real thing. It is happening every day in the life of this Miracle Man. In this particular story, there are many Spirits who were doctors in their earthly lives and who are now helping this special man heal hundreds of people daily! He is the proof that Spirits exist and do not die after their earthly death. Below is only an excerpt from the book.

The Miracle Man

We humans are strange creatures. Sometimes we see the evidence but reject the explanation, grappling instead for our own one to fit with our narrow, limited knowledge; preferably an explanation that isn't going to rock our 'conscience boat' too much, that does not require too much in the way of a radical life-change, and that does not shake the shell of security that is our understanding and perception. In light of the evidence in this book, there is no alternative explanation.

João Teixeira da Faria is the living proof. He has been tested and examined by the best scientific minds this planet can muster. He permits and welcomes these investigations in the hope that they will prove to everyone the existence of the spirit world and the importance of living correctly in this life so as to elevate ourselves in the next, instead of enduring a karmic penalty. João dedicates his life to healing the sick and incurable, without payment and without prejudice.

João Teixeira da Faria is arguably the most powerful medium alive at this time and must surely rank amongst the greatest of the past two thousand years. A "medium", as defined by the Oxford Dictionary, is a person who is "a spiritual intermediary between the living and the dead". João not only communicates with spirit, he incorporates the spirit entity; he is literally taken over by the spirit and, in doing so, loses consciousness, 'waking' a few hours later without any knowledge of his actions during the incorporation. Whilst 'in entity', his body is used as a means of conducting physical surgery and seemingly miraculous healing of the sick by the spirit entities who work through him.

João meditates in a small room at the rear of the complex before entering the main current room. To incorporate the spirit entity he simply stands before a table containing a wooden cross. He begins by asking that his hands be guided in the work of the day. Then, as he recites the Lord's Prayer, the entity enters him and takes control of his body. At the end of the daily program, he then stands up, begins a small prayer and the entity leaves his body with a visible shudder of his heavy frame. João Teixeira da Faria is a medium of extraordinary capabilities.

His mediumship enables him to take on, or incorporate, thirty-three entities, all of whom were remarkable people during their own physical lives. The entities are spirits of deceased doctors, surgeons, healers, psychologists and theologians who are of such high soul elevation they need no longer reincarnate to our physical plane. They do, however, continue to elevate in the spirit plane by the extent of their benevolence and charitable works.

João is capable of incorporating only one entity at a time, although he can change entity at any time as the need arises. It does not preclude any number of entities performing operations at the same time outside his body. During incorporation, each entity carries with him his own personality from the past life and, to those who work in the house regularly, each one can be recognized in João's behavior. (The Miracle Man: The Life Story of João de Deus, by Robert Pellegrino-Ostrich. Extracted from his book Published in 1997, ©1997/1998 All Rights Reserved).

Dream # 5
The Upper Kingdom, October 24, 1993

Part 1 – the clash

It was some terrible, black, big and hairy creature. I was feeling it. It was approaching, coming closer to me in order to kill me and some of my cute creatures, who were standing behind me, behind my back. I realized with my mind, that the beast was approaching but it was still far away. I went with my creatures to the woods, through strange brushwood, they were not woods, or bushes – they were just branches growing right out of the soil, interwoven, like barberry.... and white sand; they were growing on white sand. I brought my creatures to this THING. Then something crawled out to meet me. It had green spots all over his white body. The wise one. It appeared, suspended in front of me. It was speaking with a soft voice, like Kaa (the huge snake in the cartoon about the Indian boy, Maugli). It said to me, "I will save yours, the little ones." And it began to unwind, unroll, as if it was crawling out of an invisible crack in the wall. There was an opening and it crawled out – I didn't see the inside of the place. It was growing in size – expanding, and became as big as a Hercules plane. From the tail, a huge crack opened across its body leading my creatures inside it. Its head was flat, like a leaf. The crack was in the lower side – and my creatures started walking inside IT. And here I saw them with my eyes, I knew beforehand that I had them; that they followed me, and the snake spoke about them, but now I saw them, finally. I was very much surprised.

There were less then ten of them, maybe seven or eight. They were little animals, different from each other, sweet, nice. Spirits or Creatures... I cannot describe them. I can not even name them. Once in my dream, I went with Kaliostro – there was such a tiny elephant, and a semi-plant – None of them walked, but floated over the ground ... the spirits. They were like spirits and similar to the creatures from another dream, which looked like that little magic hen, like those two birds, which are not really birds that were coming to me, such as that shaggy-haired one that lived in my castle – that's what they looked like. Very strange, no legs, no arms, just their individual essence – very nice, very cute. Then they started walking in a line, like children in kindergarten. They did not mix up. When they were all inside it, the snake closed up, curled inside itself, slithered behind the invisible wall and disappeared.

Then suddenly this horrible beast came upon me – to kill me and my spirit-like creatures. The beast had something very sharp – something between a scythe and a sickle in its hand. Besides that, he held two more sharp things – one like the sharpest arrowhead or spearhead, a lance maybe. The second weapon was a semi-round object, similar to a fishhook, which had been inserted into a wooden stick. Once inserted into the stick, you could not pull it out. It was easier to leave it there. But it was protruding from the stick slightly. I had a feeling that it was not supposed to be put on the stick *(or it was perhaps "retractable")*, because, when you inserted the hook in it – just *a print* in a shape of the letter □□ was visible – and no one could notice it. The other weapon had a heavy ball attached to it, similar to a spiked ball attached to the end of a chain. The sharpness combined with incredible heaviness made for a dangerous weapon. It was similar to a medieval flail – a spiked ball stuck to the stick by a chain.

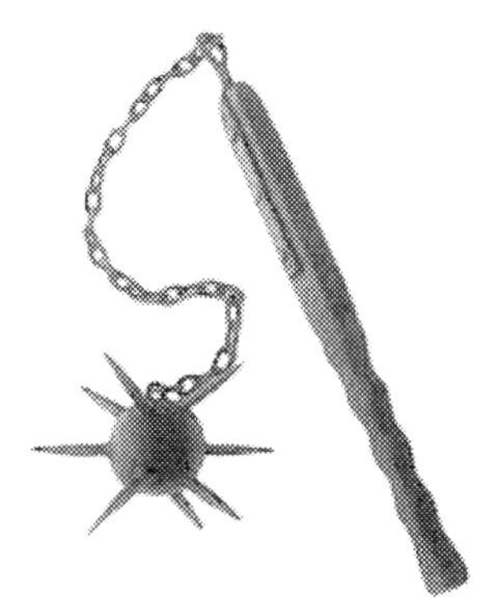

Medieval Flail

His armor was round-shaped, curved. I was rather afraid of him. I would have rather run away from him. I cannot describe him – when someone comes to kill you, then you fix your attention on the thing that is supposed to kill you. He was like a blurred, dirty, heavy, wet woolen spot – a very hairy Siberian bear; big – about two to three meters high. But I knew that I should not run away, but defend my creatures, I had to fight. Then something surprising started to happen. I was looking at everything as if from some other, second sight. Suddenly there was two of me. Everything ended up very quickly – looking from the outside – incredibly simply and easily. The other me, who was fighting did this – she was standing away at about two to three meters and then the beast lunged in my direction – at that same moment, that same second, an air stream appeared in front of him, very thin, it captured him then lunged and turned in the right direction. In front of him, there was something invisible, similar to a veil with gold threads, fibers, but incredibly taut and strong, like laser rays, twisted. There was a breath inside the veil, or something like a stream of air, invisible. This was in the air in front of him right at the moment he lunged at me with his armor. He hit the veil around him. His body was pulled into the threads, bending around and twisting to escape. It turned up, he hit, cut himself. Meanwhile, I did nothing. I just stayed there and watched from the side. Yet I knew that I had created this air-wall with threads in front of him. And I noticed that the sickle, that had stricken him and was in his hands, looked actually like a laser disc, but larger, and incredibly thin and sharp.[10]

So, when this all happened – I was surprised, but the other me, who was doing all this, went and found it

---

10 This is the kind of disks that Chak Mol had, (see the book, "Who is Chak Mol?" by Julia SvadiHatra).

immediately. She knew where to look, where it was, I felt them – the other two weapons. They were at a distance, hidden in two different places. It is hard to explain; why they were there. I approached and found the flail, without the wooden end, large – ten to fifteen centimeters long. I went to the other place and – in a strange small wooden construction, on the steps of a small house – I found a wooden box that was not touching the ground, floating in the air, just like the first weapon. While they were in such a condition, they were still dangerous – I knew this. I felt that I must level them. They could be unloaded – and I did it.

Part 2, Palace, celebration

The dream went on. After I finished with the third weapon, I went to the palace, to check what was going on there. Everything that happened occurred just before the great, magic celebration. There was to be a feast of magical enchantment with the participation of many creatures; some ritual with celebration. I was in this palace before, it is very high in the sky, and there were no more clouds. I started checking if everything was all right, everything prepared. The white columns reached to the sky as if there was no ceiling. In the center, a wide marble staircase, with white steps, suddenly emerged, like a road, stretching into the distance – so far – you could not see what was downstairs. The staircase was very wide. On the sides, there were those who were waiting for the feast to begin.

I was checking two big silver trays standing on both sides – there were strange fruit on those trays[11] – like

[11] All the way in the dream we were escorted by a guide, someone orange (later I said – of amber color), a tangerine without peel. His name was YAN, or ZWING, ZWIANG – hard to say in human language, just like some clanking sound. So this "tangerine" was possibly some Spirit, which was to be a gift to God as a

huge amber tangerines with their skin peeled away, without white particles, just little lines. But these were not tangerines, they were divine fruit. Without peel, shining through like amber – they were prepared, about ten on each tray. They were the most important items for the ritual. I started looking. While I was away to fight the monster – I could not understand how someone could commit a sacrilege – about three fruit were missing on each tray. But I was checking at the last moment, because the number of them was very important. I knew clearly, that it was a dainty piece – but not for humans. People were far away downstairs; I went to them later, for I knew the fruit was for my retinue.

There was a king in the palace. God was in the church, but he was not there, and the manager was a priest. The same as me. The symbol was a spirit, He would have come to the feast, and I was a manager, the executive. The other executives were around me. The spirit would have come, or His thoughts, or His light.... I was the lady of the kingdom. There were some creatures – not people – around me, very tall, of huge stature. The tall-sized creatures were very different, their essences were different, like the birds, the grass, as if one would have a head of an Eagle, and the other of a Snake. I knew that for some of them these dainty pieces of orange fruit were important for magic, for consecration, and maybe later they would have eaten them.

The Bold Eagle on the picture on the wall has such a beak; as if he has eaten my fruit... An eagle with its sharp beak can pick, peel and swallow them up very quickly.

---

sacrifice. But maybe it was just an ancient fruit, which doesn't exist anymore.

In short, I noticed it, I checked the fruits that were left and went downstairs to the people. But maybe, because there were not enough of them, they were losing their quality, and they did not have the same quality together. So I gave both trays to the people around me. Maybe they had eaten them. I went down the stairs. Downward, the staircase opened wide, like in Rome's amphitheatres, and at the open side there was a stormy ocean. It was a sunny day. I was up on the columns, talking – up there, where the stairs were coming together with the upper colonnade like amphitheatre. There were crowds of people downstairs. They all were wearing strange clothes – ancient Roman togas, and fabrics fastened by a buckle on the shoulder, and in short iron skirts, in chain armor – all different designs. But there were no wild ones, everybody was normal. They were standing in the amphitheatre, and on the beach – but they were not swimming, not sunbathing. I was looking at the sea – the sea was important. It was stormy, I looked carefully – it was dangerous. It was boiling from something inside it. Some herds were coming out of it by groups – some elephants, and other creatures. They were not animals. I went down. When I found myself in some narrow corridor just before the amphitheatre, I saw that some new creatures began to appear from the ocean – they were some kind of deer, or rather goats – a huge mass, they were walking very closely to each other – horns, hooves, many hooves. And I understood, that it became dangerous – many hooves. They were coming one after another, you could not stop them. And then I told to my surrounding to leave. Actually, I was not talking – I had a sign. But in that corridor people were running towards me – they all were rushing to the ocean. I was telling them, that it is dangerous, "don't do it" – but they were running, and blocking my way and the way of my people up... I don't remember, what happened afterwards...

"So those goat-deer disturbed your celebration?"

Not at all. It is like if you prepare yourself for a feast, invite some guests, and then in a free moment, you go to the window to look outside – I was watching the scene from somewhere above it.

I saw this statue on the beach on the sand in Acumal, Riviera Maya, and it reminded me about this dream and this goat-deer, unusual animal with many hooves. Maybe they existed 10,000 years ago?

Animals with hooves from the ocean

The Priest

Bas relief sculpture in Chichen Itza showing captive rulers or nobles involved in a ritual ceremony.

When I saw this picture in the book "The Origin of the Advanced Maya Civilization in the Yucatan", by Douglas T. Peck, I was truly amazed! Because this ancient picture on the wall of Chichen Itza was portraying exactly the four people, including me, who were in that sacrifice ceremony! From left, there was a SNAKE, next an EAGLE and next, ANUBIS, and the Priest JAGUAR stood on the right – they were my "colleagues."

I don't think they were captive; this is the position these nobles assumed right before the ritual ceremony. In my vision, following the hypnosis sessions, I remember how each of us had a very thin rope and string in our hands to fill at first with our own energy, and afterwards we traced a circle and connected these ropes with each other through the top layer of the skin up to the navel area. We needed to be ALL as ONE at the same time. Each of us had a little blood trickling onto this rope, coming from the skin and our blood was then mixed....

When you read this, you may have a clear picture of what I describe and what you think about it.... You may ask, "Why are they doing this? Are they insane maybe?"

No, I found that they were smarter than we are – they were wise. What we just discovered now, using the most advanced science is what these people knew and used successfully in their daily lives thousands of years ago.

After we prayed and supported each other with combined energy, we had the ability to talk to Spirits, to GOD, and maybe check the Hall of Records for information about the Past and Future or maybe just talk to our "colleagues" from Egypt, and decided on some kind of trivial question regarding experience or technical support. For example, we could ask how to build a pyramid – some kind of teleconference with knowledge exchange.

I called Europe today and talked to the famous scientist, Peter Gariaev, the father of wave genetic. Here is how he explained this ritual:

DNA phantoms can be perceived as means of genetic-metabolic communications between organisms on the wave level. It is something like "immaculate conception". DNA not only passes information in a form of wave replicas, but it also records information from the environment (replicas of the parts of apparatus, lamp). Thus the replicas get to know the surrounding and translate this information onto genetic level in the chromosomes, the organism, alienating probe-replicas and returning back to the organism with new knowledge. People united by a "blood rope" form a hyper-personality; build an antenna and become the acceptors of information from OUTSIDE, the Universe – alien visitors maybe. They are capable of assimilating it because they are all united by the common quantum entangled blood of each other and because of that, being a hyper-personality; they are capable to accomplish something much bigger, together and then separately. For those interested in studying the subject, he advises to read also the article "Quantum Magic" by S.I. Doronin.

DNA Found to Have "Impossible" Telepathic Properties, Journal of Physical Chemistry B, Geoff S. Baldwin, Sergey Leikin, John M. Seddon, and Alexei A. Kornyshev. DNA has been found to have a bizarre ability to put itself together, even at a distance, when according to known science, it shouldn't be able to do so. Explanation: None, at least not yet.

Scientists are reporting evidence that contrary to our current beliefs about what is possible, intact double-stranded DNA has the "amazing" ability to recognize similarities in other DNA strands from a distance. Somehow they are able to identify one another, and the tiny bits of genetic material tend to congregate with similar DNA. The recognition of similar sequences in DNA's chemical sub-units, occurs in a way unrecognized by science. There is no known reason why the DNA is able to combine the way it does, and from a current theoretical standpoint this feat should be chemically impossible.

Strands with identical nucleotide sequences were about twice as likely to gather together as DNA strands with different sequences. No one knows how individual DNA strands could possibly be communicating in this way, yet somehow they do. The "telepathic" effect is a source of wonder and amazement for scientists. (You will find more details of scientific explanation at the end of the book)

In their book "Vernetzte Intelligenz" (Networked Intelligence), Grazyna Fosar and Franz Bludorf explain these connections precisely and clearly. The authors also quote sources, presuming that in earlier times, humanity had been, just like the animals, very strongly connected to the group consciousness and acted as a group. To develop and experience individuality we, humans, however, had to forget hyper-communication almost completely. [12]

Interesting that when I was a Priest, I accepted all people around me like my close relatives. Now I find that in those times, the Mayan people had marriages between close relatives, so finally the whole village was one big family! According to genetics, I know that this is not a good idea; it creates some side effects that could be inherited and dangerous for the wellbeing of the

---

[12] You will find DNA phantoms and Scientific Interpretations with more details about this at the end of the book.
Here is how a few authors try to explain rituals involving blood and sacrifices: “Maya worldview was a vision of vast cycles or cosmic spirals of time, embodied and expressed by seething pantheon of extravagant deities, hero-twins, and cosmic monsters. Trained in shamanic practices and initiatory disciplines, members of the nobility were thought to be able to contact there entities directly. These nonhuman entities required appeasement - sometimes through the blood - and could be directly evoked in shamanic trance states.” “For the ancient Maya, human beings released their *ch'ulel* (soul-stuff) from their bodies when they left their blood. Through bloodletting, they “conjured” (tzak) the *way* and *the ch'u,the* 'companion spirit and gods,” wrote David Freidel, Linda Schele, and Joy Parker in *Maya Cosmos*. Pinchbeck, 2012 The return of Quetzalcoatl, 2006
If the “Galactic Maya” had space-time-tripped to Earth from Hunab Ku, the Galactic Center, this did not happened through cumbersome rockets, but through “harmonic resonance”, pattern of genetic information intentionally transmitted from start to star, encoded in light a “wave-harmonic means of transmission, communication, and passing from one condition of being to another. The “so-called sun worship” of the Maya and ancient Egypt was actually “the recognition and acknowledgment that higher knowledge and wisdom is literally being transmitted through the Sun, or more precisely, through the cycles of the binary sunspot movements.”

children. However, this kind of connection may be giving life-saving opportunities with rare important information.

Ancient Maya had a common type of marriage, called cross-cousin. The familial clan was presented by constantly intersecting lines of cousin sisters and brothers, thus all members of the clan had common ancestors, beginning with grandfathers More than that, every second generation names of these relatives by female ancestral line were repeated. Thus, for instance, maternal grandfather, brother of wife and grandson by a daughter were called the same name: mum. The same word represented mythical forefather of Maya. In this way all men of the clan by ritual mixing of their blood were tied up together and with their forefather, divine Mum. (Ref. 29 “Ancient America: Flight in time and prostransive. Mezoamerika” Excerpts from the book by GG Ershovoy UnCopyrighted©Sam, 2003-2006)

Dream # 6
The Queen of a Crystal Kingdom, December 4, 2007

It was a strange dream. I got to bed at 11:50pm, and woke up at 2:30am. Then the dream continued. There were three parts to it.

1. First Kingdom It was like they were preparing me. They sucked out every material out of me, piece by piece. They were purifying me. They pulled out everything from inside my body. I became as light as a bubble, and transparent. They were doing some rituals with me. After purification I entered the Kingdom of Transition. It was more structured than mine was. It consisted of two huge spaces. I was in one of them, and in the other, there was God – an old man, speaking in human language. I understood that he was a Master here. I was afraid to move, to take a step, to break anything, to spoil anything by my presence here. He also did something to me, some ritual with a space, maybe with clouds. We were talking (he was speaking, and I was listening). He did not leave His territory. Afterwards, I was ready – all my psychic structures were ready. For in my next Kingdom it was much finer. They moved me to this 2nd kingdom after the ritual was completed. They were purifying me, in a way, but they could not enter the place themselves.

2. Crystal spaces The first sensation – there is ice everywhere. Everything is transparent. The person becomes like a blue-gray colloid. Large crystals – all made of ice – like finely streamlined ... such a pleasant bliss. I was alone. And they told me – in my mind – that I am a tsarina in this kingdom. Well in our language the words tzarstvo (kingdom) – they are bulky, sharp, and heavy. But there – everything was like air, harmonious, beautiful. Everything here was perfection itself, completeness. Nothing in excess. All was completed, when I was brought in. I felt "complete" – I was full.

At the beginning I was getting accustomed – everything was light-blue-crystal-clear-turquoise. But there was a feeling, that all this was frosted, sparkling with snowflakes. The kingdom was similar to the huge stadium-sphere in Vancouver, as if the kingdom was situated in the sphere.

3. Alexandrian and New York kingdoms I went down by the sphere – and I saw beside me some elevation on one side and on the other. In one of the spheres an old lady appeared – like that old man from Indiana Jones, who was guarding the water of life. Her arms and legs were not visible; her body appeared to be just a stream of veils beneath her head. She said, "These two Kingdoms are Alexandrian and New York. They are your assistants. They can fly over to you from their places –

two persons, two souls." I could address them as my assistants, my secretaries. They are the two lightest spirits from those kingdoms.[13]

Dream # 7
Arabian and American Mountains - 2 pyramids: Egypt and Mexico, October 25, 1990

I was escorted by a laden-gray doughnut, of a strange square-round shape – either round outside and square inside or vice-versa.[14] There were mountains in front of me. The voice in my ear, this doughnut-guide reported: "Arabian peninsula..." and was telling me about the future of this place, what it is called now, how it will be called, what will go where, which people will pass by, and which will die. *He* was speaking from over my head and his voice was enveloping me. The mountain in front of me was not material, but maybe made of psychic emanations from the people assembled in the shape of a pyramid. And right after that we flew to America, to the other mountain – also a pyramid. Both pyramids are located on the same latitude.[15] *When you fly over an area you can't remember rivers, lakes, seas, but you can remember the similarities between two places.* The doughnut-guide was with me all the time.

---

[13] I understood it not as a New York City, but some new city, so Alexandria was the old city, built earlier. I think there were two sets of pyramids, the ones in Egypt (Alexandrian) and the second one in Mexico, New York being a new city.

[14] Another famous Egyptologist, Arnold de Belizal, later inherited the ring. He was a well-known expert in radio-aesthesia, the science concerned with the energy of shapes. De Belizal's found that the ring emits electromagnetic waves capable of creating 'energy fields' which work as a force of energy. This energy protected the wearer, gave him increased psychic abilities and the ability to heal, and brought the person good luck. The Atlantis Ring, http://www.crystalinks.com/atlantisring.html

[15] Both pyramids, in Egypt and Mexico, are on the same latitude.

His voice was talking to me very quickly – humans cannot talk that fast – it was saying different things, which I could not memorize. The views were replacing each other, the voice followed with information – very even; all phrases were similar, spoken like a robot. The letters were like little beads tumbling down through my ears at incredible speed. It was impossible to understand the meaning, if there are no mistakes in the speech and no human details. I mean when there is no timber or inflection, pauses, tonality, etc. in the voice; you cannot understand what the person is saying. One view was followed by another followed by the text. When I said "stop" to myself, in order to memorize and put fragments together, I was confused; I lost the train of thought. I worried. And I even forgot this. When I started to try to fly from one mountain to the other – slowly, since slowly is what I could remember, the voice began talking more slowly, 5 to 10 times more slowly. There was a feeling that it was speaking through water. The words came to me evenly and clearly.

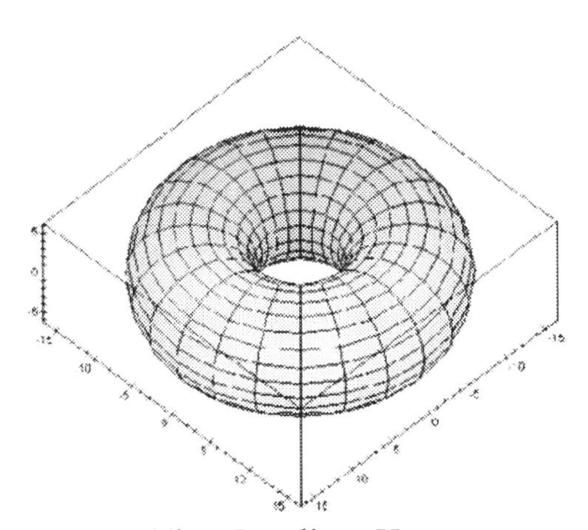

The Gordian Knot

The Priest

Science began using this model and, THIS is what I meant in my dream!
http://www.crystalinks.com/gordianknot.html

Sacred geometry: - an ancient mystery schools teaching, stressed the one force or consciousness behind existence through the laws of geometry, made extensive. According to ancient teachings in the beginning there was a great void. This void is the creator, with no body shape or definition. Creation requires a definition of space (as well as direction). The Torus tube provides this kind of definition by using the inside, the outside, and infinity. In that way it can be the shape that also represents the idea of The one and only God and the holy trinity relation, which comes from the one God and exists in everything (positive, negative and neutral, for example). The word "one" in Hebrew, "Echad" as well as the word "love" – "Ahava" in Hebrew, has a numerological value of 13. The number 13 contains the one and the three. [1+3=4=time].

Many people claim they had dreams in which they were able to solve difficult karmatic personal relations or situations during the daytime after wearing a Gordian knot pendant. The reason for this might be that the pendant symbolizes the idea of unity which binds everything into one.
- Wikipedia: http://en.wikipedia.org/wiki/Knot_theory

I find one more website with Sacred Geometry: www.akaija.com. The Akaija is a cosmic jewel made in co-operation with the Divine Lightworld. Wim Roskam, the maker of the Akaija, has been given this object by his girlfriend Linda, who died in 2001. She was sending him many dimensional images and inspired him to start producing them as jewelry! This jewelry carries amazing power!

http://www.ka-gold-jewelry.com/p-products/gordian-knot-silver-big.php#ProDetails

Akaija = The Oneness of 'We'

Now look at the name: Akaija. When you analyze 'akaija' numerologically something strange is found: every character in the alphabet stands for a number. In that way the A stands for 1, B for 2, C for 3, etc. 'Akaija' has a rare combination of numbers: A=1, K=11, A=1, IJ = I+J = 9+10 = 19 = 1+9 = 10 = 1+0 = 1 and A=1. One character splits into two numbers 1, and two characters (I+J), merge into one number 1, fission and fusion. This way you get: 1 + 11 + 1 + 1 + 1, so six ones. The 5th dimension (5 characters) upgrades to the 6th dimension (6 numbers). Six represents the planet Venus, and stands for Love. And funny as it was... the moment I wrote this down for the first time I saw the clock on the computer: 11:11. Putting together these data (Akaija=We and Akaija=111111) a very clear and not to misunderstand message comes out: WE, every-1, every individual together, are ONE!!!

Interesting too are the symbols that can be found in the Akaija. Depending on how you look at it, you discover several symbols: a circle, a yin-yang-symbol, a 5-pointed star (pentagram), and a Heart that is protected by the Circle, but due to the Akaija's special construction it also protects the Circle. 'We', the Never-Ending-Circle, protect your heart, and 'We' connect you to the Endless Love, which is the basis of our relation of our existence. 'We' show you that You are never al-one, but all-one. Put it this way: We are the Universe, and the Akaija symbolizes universal Love.

http://www.akaija.com/info/UK/UK06_3D.shtml
http://www.akaija.com/info/UK/UK05_gallery.shtml

Akaija symbolizes universal Love.

Dream # 8
I return to the land where I lived before, November 13, 1992

This is a short version of the dream. It was about me arriving to America, Mexico. In my dream I walked on this land and my grandmother tells me that this is the land where I was living before.... When we were driving through Canada, from Toronto to Vancouver, during the night in the prairies, I started feeling that some spirit was near me. I knew at that moment that this was a native Indian spirit, who owns all of this land... I started talking to him and asked permission – it's a blessing to settle down in this North American land.

The other day, I was under a hot shower – I love hot showers – and I started remembering that I had this dream, and suddenly I was covered with goose bumps – like a hoar-frost covering my skin – under a hot shower! I was shaking. It was surprising to me to feel frozen under a hot shower!

I never had such goose bumps, so often, such as I had this spring while I was writing this book and reading the dreams which I collected over the years. The energy was coded in the words of the dreams. When Di Cherry started reading my dreams, while I was under hypnosis, the doors of the past opened for me instantly. I could see, feel, smell, and touch such as I did all those years ago. Psychic people know that when something real comes from the past or another side of life, they are often covered with goose bumps.

****

Today I received an envelope from Dr. Alfons Ven from Holland with the custom-made pills – made especially for me. I am totally healthy; these are really "miracle pills".

I opened the instructions and read this magic sentence: *The aim of the Ven-Cure is to elicit a better attunement with your evolution and being freer with your original selves.* When I was reading those words, I was near a window, looking at cherry blossoms, pink rhododendrons and brand new emerald-green leaves on an apple tree, and I started smiling... It was a very unusual smile, which I never experienced in my life. I wish I could have watched myself from the side. I was very surprised.

I have no words to describe what I really felt. There were waves of the wise, heavenly, and beautiful – the kindest, softest sort of energy – invading me such as a tide of happiness and contentment, and it was coming out with this smile through my eyes. I continued looking at the flowers and continued to smile blissfully. It was an astonishing pleasure to feel God's touch. It was something amazing and unusual! I wish I had a witness to this magical experience at that moment or a video camera to record the look in my eyes. I wish that someone saw it and told me what it looked like.

I decided to keep these miraculous, pure lactose pills near my pillow. When I look at them from the side right now, they look like little lilies-of-the-valley or snow-drop flowers – they're the cutest round, white balls. I feel harmony and connection with this special, beautiful, glowing energy, which makes them so appealing. I know why! They have my own pure energy from heaven, which GOD gave me at the moment He created me. They connect me with God and will guide me to return to my own original self. I think everyone should make such an adjustment once during their lifetime with Dr. Alfons Ven's unique help.

****

I read an interesting article: "Organ Transplants and Cellular Memories".

Here is how it starts:
"According to this study, for patients, who have received transplanted organs, particularly hearts, it is not uncommon for memories, behaviors, preferences and habits associated with the donor to be transferred to the recipient. If you wish to upset the law that all crows are black...it is enough if you prove one single crow to be white," William James, M.D.

There are many cases of people who have received skills and habits from the previous owner of the heart, together with the heart transplant because all living cells have "memory". The first case reported was that of a boy who was killed in an automobile accident. The recipient was an 18-year-old girl. They never knew and never saw each other. After his death, a year later, his parents found a song while cleaning their son's room. He had entitled the song: "Danny, My Heart Is Yours".

"The words are about how my son felt he was destined to die and give his heart to someone. It has left us shaken emotionally and spiritually," his father told me. This boy was writing poems and songs. The name of the girl who received his heart was Danny! She started writing poems and songs after the operation! Here is what she said, *"When they showed me pictures of their son, I knew him directly. I would have picked him out anywhere. I know he is in me and he is in love with me. How could he know years before he died that he would die and give his heart to me? How would he know my name is Danny? And then, when they played me some of his music, I could finish the phrases of his songs. I could never play before, but after my transplant I began to love music. I felt it in my heart. My heart had to play it. I told my mom I wanted to take guitar lessons – the same instrument Paul (the donor) had played. His song is in me. I feel it a lot at night and it's like Paul is serenading me."*

I am thinking about all of this, because I find lots of things in common between the Priest and me. I am sure there will be a list of items in your present life that you will be able to compare with those of your past lives. The next pages should enable you to see that we not only have genes from our real relatives, but also that our personality is strongly affected by our previous life. My idea is simple: people have genes which carry some skills, abilities; we can have cellular memories from our mother and father, since we are built from their cells, but we also have spirit memories from our past lives. People collect many skills and experiences from their past life which they can use in their present and future lives. What we are developing now will be useful in our next lives.

When I was studying plants during my post-graduate courses, my teacher was an 85-year-old professor, academician A. A. Prokofiev. I was his last student in this life. When this extremely smart, amazingly wise man died, on top of the deep sorrow and sadness I felt, I had one thought, which always came to my mind that day: "How unfair that people exercise their brain throughout their lives and when it is rich and at the highest point in its development, the person dies and all of these skills are lost forever." Now I know that nothing is lost and that these skills will be transferred with the Spirit to his next life.

There are many cases of talented, gifted people who were born with rare skills which they were able to apply from a very young age, such as Connie Talbot, Akiane Kramarik, Joshua Johnson, Carlos Blanco, the world's most talented kids. (Akiane Kramarik
http://www.artakiane.com)
http://www.tagtele.com/videos/voir/19214/1/Connie

I remember arriving once at Di Cherry's office and meeting a pretty Chinese girl who had just finished a past life hypnosis session. She found that in her past life she lived in England. This fact may explain why, when she moved to Canada, she started talking in pure

English without any accent – just a few months after her arrival.[16]

Here is a page from the book, the "Miracle man" with some of the most important, basic knowledge about the nature of our own Spirit and the Spirit world.

1) *"We have all lived many lives before this one. We are incarnated, and after this life we will be reincarnated again into another life. (There are many well-documented cases of hypnotists taking countless numbers of people back into past lives. They speak languages totally foreign to them and they describe in detail places and lifestyles of long ago, which are frequently proven correct by subsequent investigation.)*
2) *If you remove the physical shell we call the body, what is left is the real you: your soul, your spirit. This eternal essence is in a perpetual state of improvement or deterioration, depending on what you do in each of your physical lives.*
3) *Free will is the only means by which the physical you, and subsequently your soul, can improve its position after your demise.*
4) *Karma is the means by which you will pay your debt for wrongdoings or be rewarded for your free-will choice of good in each life. If you have killed, stolen, lied or cheated in a past life, chances are that you will be suffering some malady or conflict in your current life. Conversely, if you have been caring, considerate, honest and moral, then your soul will have elevated and you will probably be a healthy, well-balanced person.*
5) *There is a spirit world! It is much more complex than our physical world. It is much more powerful and decidedly more beautiful for those who have earned a*

[16] You will find more scientific details about gene memory transfers at the end of the book, "The Re-birth of an Atlantean Queen, by Julia SvadiHatra.

place in it. It is multi-leveled and multidimensional, to cater for the infinite number of development stages through which souls pass. Of over 150 out-of-body, near-death experiences surveyed by Kenneth Ring (author of Heading Towards Omega: In Search of the Meanings of Near-Death Experience), all reported similar observations, feelings and experiences to support this belief.

6) *Spirits, both good and bad, are with us all the time. So many of those strange coincidences we experience (usually when we most earnestly wish for them) are the result of thought generation picked up and acted upon by your guides, your spirit guides. It adds new meaning to the biblical quotation, "Ask and ye shall receive".*
7) *Our human bodies are generated from and protected by energy fields. There are seven corresponding layers, each with its own density or frequency, and seven major chakras (spinning vortexes). Some people can actually see these layers as auras. If we live healthy, clean lives, our energy fields protect us very well. Conversely, if we abuse ourselves with excesses of alcohol, drugs or unclean living, the fields become weakened, will be attacked and will attract undesirable attachments. Disease begins in these outer layers and the fields lose their vibrancy.*

In one of the room, dressed in white, sit twenty to thirty mediums in meditation. This meditation provides the current to assist the entities in their work. Interestingly, in the Edgar Cayce readings on Atlantis, there is a reference to this type of combined energy used by the Atlanteans to achieve their extraordinarily advanced civilization; a similar production of spiritual current.

The second current room contains fifty or more mediums similarly seated in rows. The endless line of people pass through the middle and are spiritually prepared to meet

João-in-entity who sits at the far end in a large chair covered in white linen. At the moment of meeting there is a split-second recognition by the entity of each person's 'blueprint': past lives, current situation, illness and spiritual awareness. Depending on what is seen, the person will be dealt with according to the requirement. Some are given herbal prescriptions. Some are sent to the intensive care room for surgery or treatment at a later time. Those who need spiritual strength may be told to sit in current, whilst others are given concise instructions on necessary life changes. Each person is dealt with in less than twenty seconds.

Here is a list of "inheritance", which Spirit, who lives in my body, got from past life as a Priest. I guarantee that you will find some of these "habits" crazy or at least shocking.

Anyway, in this life the Priest's Spirit continues his habits:

1. Ball court & Basketball,
2. Healing,
3. Intuition, Predictions,
4. Jaguar pattern outfits,
5. Leadership,
6. Astrology,
7. Numbers,
8. Plants, Agriculture,
9. Masks,
10. Caracol – the observatory,
11. Aztek God Xochipilli,
12. I always wanted to be Priest!
13. Tortoise,
14. Connection with the Goddess Bodhisattva, Meeting with God,
15. Ghosts.

1. Ball court & Basketball

When I was in school, I tried avoiding gymnastic classes as much as possible. I think it is wrong for ordinary kids, who did not attend any special training to participate in gymnastic classes. I am sure school gymnastic often leads to injury. Anyway, the only thing, which helped me survive and keep my grades, was basketball. But it is not only a game in itself.

Our teacher, Margarita Stepanovna, asked each of us to take the ball and throw it up to the basket 10 times and then she would grade our performance. When it was my turn, my classmates ran to watch me throw the ball. I could throw the ball into the basket 10, 20, 40 times, without fail. The ball always went through the hoop easily. In the end, our teacher said, "Okay, enough!" But my classmates were screaming for me to be allowed to continue. All of the kids in school and my neighbors knew about my talent. I guess the Priest's spirit remembered how he played in the ball court in Chichen Itza, only a few thousand years ago. Believe me; it is much easier to do this with your hands than with the knees and elbows, such as the ancient Maya players did.

By the way, I always thought that this basketball hoop should be turned to the side, such as I saw it in the ball court in Chichen Itza. It's much more comfortable and everyone will agree with me. The ancient Mayas knew what they were doing, and did it very well.

2. Healing

The Priest applied his healing power to his people often. I always paid attention, asked about the health of each person around me and gave advice. Today, it comes out automatically as if I have some program set up inside me to do this. Interesting that I catch myself many times, scanning people's health during my dreams and I heal them. I care about all of my business partners' wellbeing. I try to keep all of them in good health while preventing them from catching some diseases with homeopathy, herbal treatments and advice.

3. Intuition, predictions

I am sure the Priest had stronger intuitions, with his hyper-communication ability and being in harmony with nature, than I ever did. I got good intuition too. I got it as an "inheritance" from him. I had lots of predictions about big events, which have come true.

Once, I woke up deeply depressed. I saw, in my dream, the horror of the Twin Towers' collapse in all of its disastrous details – I was right there. It was exactly one year before it happened. I told the people around me at the time, and one replied to me, saying, "There was an explosion under a building a few years ago. This is what you saw in your dream."

On September 11, 2001, I was walking through a little street in Rarotonga, Cook Islands in the middle of the South Pacific Ocean. The local doctor, Wolfgang, who was also the German consul there, waved at me from his office and said, "I was rushed to work today and I saw on TV that a small airplane hit one of the Twin Towers in New York."

I asked him, "Have both building already collapsed?" He looked at me curiously and replied, "How can you even imagine this – two huge, concrete buildings will collapse?"

I said, "If they are not both destroyed yet, they will be soon and there will only be debris left." I remembered wishing that I could have said to him, "I know it, because I saw it in my dream...," but I just walked across the street to the internet café. Letters had arrived already from everyone: "Remember what you said about the Twin Towers? Terrible things have happened...." In those days, in Cook Islands news arrived late – at least 12 hours or a day late....

I remember how I woke up around 4:00am one morning and told my grandmother: "Indira Gandhi has just been killed – right now!" I found out later that she had indeed died on October 31, 1984. The dream had occurred at the exact moment when the Indian Prime Minister, Indira Gandhi, had been assassinated. I liked her!

I woke up from a dream about a huge earthquake in Armenia. I saw trucks full of frozen, dead bodies. People were sliding the corpses into the trucks as if they were on an ice sheet after they had pushed them inside. About 100,000 people died in that terrible, devastating earthquake. It happened the day after I had the dream.

Once, I started writing my dreams on a list, where I only noted the predictions as I saw them in each dream. I wrote the list down in November 1991. When I had about 30 of them, I stopped. All 30 came true. They all happened during the next one and half to two months afterwards. I marked near each one: *happened, come true today,* etc. and *Wow – this one also happened!* And so on....

I try avoiding seeing the future; because of dramatic events. I avoid looking at people's faces, because, some days, I can see how they will die. I check the future only when it is really necessary. For example, I often see in my dreams what will happen the same day or the next.

Once, we needed to travel 1500km in one day by car. This was a long road.... When I woke up early that morning, I started envisioning the road. I saw a crossing, where the roads in all directions were covered with a red liquid. "How could an accident create so much blood?" I asked myself. I was worried. We arrived at the crossing at nightfall. The roads were indeed covered with the blood . . . of tomatoes! There had been an accident at this intersection earlier that day. A huge truck full of boxes of tomatoes had turned over on its side, spilling its entire content on the road! Before the truck had been hauled off from the site, many cars had passed through smashed tomatoes. There was juice everywhere. This was a funny case of prediction turning out all right.

Another time, we were to travel through Poland. When I started checking the road ahead in my mind, I heard a screeching metal sound. I had no idea what it could be – except perhaps my car was going to be dragged during an accident. When we drove that day, the front license plate fell down to the side, scratched the surface of the road, and began making the same screeching, horrible sound as the one I had heard before leaving on our trip.

4. Jaguar

From a very young age, the jaguar has always been my favorite animal. Today, I favor the jaguar pattern in any of the clothes I buy. It makes me feel very comfortable – as if it were my own skin. I guess when the priest was wearing his jaguar coat for forty or fifty years, it created a DNA phantom, which seeped through and into the "cellular memory" of his Spirit.[17].

---

[17] It sounds really strange, but if you are interested, please read the scientific part, with the latest research at the end of the book. It will clarify some of the questions you may have on the subject, I'm sure.

I am also attracted to the animal's movements and energy flow. The jaguar moves are often associated with ancient martial arts such as Kung Fu. When people come to me, asking for help with the Kung Fu association in the former Soviet Union, I agree instantly. In fact, I helped legalizing the first martial art, Kung Fu & Tai Chi Association in the country. Martial arts had been illegal and prohibited for 70 years. I was even Vice President of this association in Moscow!

5. Leadership

This martial arts association was the first independent, private sports' association in the country when PERESTROIKA and democracy began to emerge in Russia. I had a big fight with the Sports Committee who had kept sports' people on a small salary and used to collect all of the money from the Olympic Games. Finally they agreed, but with the condition that the president would be a former KGB general! When I went to China for the competition with the first group, he tried to close the association. As soon as I returned I called a big meeting with all the masters – thousands attended the meeting.
I asked those present: "Do we need a president like this? NO!" They agreed. I then turned to the former KGB general and told him, "You're free to go...." And he left.

The world chess champion, Garry Kasparov, was the first who came to us and asked for advice. "How did you do it?" he asked. "I wish to open a school for the children and teach them how to play." Hockey, chess, soccer, and many other sports' associations followed in our footsteps afterwards. I was part of the sports' "elite" then and flew first class with the hockey player, Tretiak, to Canada. Today, in Russia, millions of people study

Martial Arts. In Moscow alone, my Kung Fu Association counts over 50 thousand members. I helped them and as soon as they were stable on their "legs", I left this association to help others.

The organization skills I had acquired during my life as a Priest and leader were used in this present life.

6. Astrology

Astrology was a very important part of the Priest's daily life.
I never believed in astrology until a famous astrologer predicted my future and everything came true! As a scientist, I wished to understand how it was possible. Therefore, I decided to study it a little and now I understand the main principles. By the way, Astrology was also illegal for 70 years in the former Soviet Union. Many things were illegal then, even such things as innocent as astrology. I was the leader who opened the door for astrology and created the first association in Russia.

When we published our first astrology book about Nostradamus and another six most famous astrologers, with their predictions, instead of my real name I used the pen name "Magician". I didn't have any idea what it meant in those days – remember the Russian alphabet is quite different than our alphabet – and for me to compose such a name meant that it must have been imprinted in my "memory" beforehand. I just didn't feel comfortable with my own last name, it did not sound right for this book. So I used the word, "Magician". I wrote it letter by letter from my mind, because I felt in harmony with this word. I even took my membership in the astrology association under this name. A few months ago, I found that the name "Magician" was used to designate the Highest Priests in ancient Mexico!

The Priest

When I was due to give birth to my daughter, I consulted the charts and noticed that if she were to be born on July 4, her horoscope would not be that great. So, I decided to delay her birth by a couple of weeks and turned the clock back until the time was right. She was born on July 21 with a fabulous astrology chart. Each planet in her chart was in the strongest, most powerful configuration.

There are planets that stay in their own particular place – the Moon, Venus, Jupiter, Saturn, Uranus, and Neptune. These planets are inscribed in a perfect hexagram – an extremely favorable aspect. This hexagram connects all of the planets on the map, and not one stands out of it. Long before now, this hexagram represented the key principle of the Universe – harmony and balance. Regulus, the star of the kings, is a guiding star for it. Very rare. It looks like a perfect star. In fact, my daughter's chart is always a big surprise to astrologers. And it looks like it helped her! From the day she was born, she could keep her head straight! Usually, children can't do this until they are one and half or two months old. But the most amazing thing to me was that she was able to stand instantly on her legs! She just needed to hold my hand a little bit for balance. The nurse, who gave her the first immunization shots, was speechless... "Usually, kids start to stand at eight or ten months," she said. She also told me that I should apply for the Genius Record. (I still have pictures and video.)

My daughter started reading by herself when she was two and half years old. No one taught her to read. Once I went out with her and she started reading the names of all the stores around the mall. I asked her how come she could read. She replied, "Remember I asked you to read me every evening a fairy tale story and you sometimes were too busy? You told me that if I knew my letters, I could read anything in the world. I was very happy that evening and I started studying...."

Such a serious child for a 3-year-old!
She has adult eyes here...

I remember after her first day in kindergarten, the teacher stopped me and said, "Your daughter ... your daughter...," I asked her, "What's wrong?" She then told me that my five-year-old girl brought "The Lord of the Rings" with her to school and was reading the entire day! The teacher was amazed that a child of that age could read so fast when other kids don't even know their alphabet and cannot read.

A few days later the teacher asked me to go and see the principal. He said that my daughter already went through all of the school programs up to 4th grade! At age five, she had finished the computer programs – preschool format, kindergarten schooling, and that she had completed grade 1, 2, 3 and 4 tests successfully! I asked the principal to put her in grade 5, but since she was only five years old, he told me, that she would feel very uncomfortable studying with the older kids. At that point, I wanted to find out how she was studying and how she could have attained such an intellectual level so rapidly.

Her playthings and toys consisted mainly of a computer that I had put in front of her when she was only 17 months old. She received many study games and toys that developed her brain very early. Her first game was Catz. In this game, there were cats which she could feed, paint, and play with. It was very interesting to see a child, who couldn't talk yet – from the way she was doing things on the computer – you would know how a child at this age was thinking. Every outline and everything was different: the way she was drawing, playing with her cats, feeding them, painting them, put clothes on them or hunting for the mouse with 30 water sprays or build a wall from hundreds of pillows!

Soon she started to be attached to this game, so much so, that she would run to the computer as soon as she woke up, stop paying attention to the adults around her, and only contact her animals in the computer – because for each movement of the mouse, the animals reacted to her. One morning, I deleted the game from her computer. After a few days, she was playing again! She couldn't read yet, but she went through the network to Shawn's computer and found the game by remembering what the letters looked like and downloaded the program onto her computer. It was unbelievable. Yet I could not deny the fact that my daughter was playing with her favorite game again.

My business partners were amazed with her memory ability when, at age seven, in London, she started listing each capital city in each country of the world.

Last week, now 13 years old, she was a gold medal a winner in geography, coming first in front of all the kids, up to grade 12, from the whole of Vancouver.

Once at age eight, in Los Angeles, when a translator was sick, she translated the whole day's business meetings for the airline company regarding equipment for the airplanes. People were amazed at her level of concentration and her ability to study airplane parts instantly, while putting her knowledge in English to build an order. The Los Angeles Company then gave her a huge gift: she visited Disney Land during the next five days. On one of the days, Donald Nixon, the co-owner of Disney Land and nephew of Richard Nixon, personally went through all of the best attractions with her, sometimes carrying her on his shoulders. Afterwards, he invited us for dinner in Walt Disney's private restaurant.

7. Numbers

a. Interesting that the Priest decided to be re-born in this present life where the day, year, hour and minute comprised only the numbers 8 and 5. Birthday numbers have only 8 and 5 for the year, 8 for the day, and 5:58 for the hour and minutes. When I got the original ISBN for my book, The Priest, I noticed the last numbers: 108-5-8 which is the 10th month – October, 8 – the day, 5 and 8 are the numbers of the year I was born.

Year 2008, according to the Maya calendar, is year 5008. This is the year when I found my past life as a Maya Priest and visited Mexico for the first time. Meaning of #5 and #8: The Priest, The Hand of God, Body and Soul.

In Mayan contexts, each number from one to nine had a sacred value, and since the Mayan number system was based on the number 20, there is given meanings to numbers, and the figures and patterns that they were inscribed upon:

1. *God, Goddess*
2. *The Maker, Parents*
3. *The Created, Life*
4. *Venus, called Kukulcan*
5. *The Priest, The Hand of God*
6. *Life and Death*
7. *God and Divine Power*
8. *Body and Soul*
9. *The Nine Drinks*

What we do know is that these patterns were carved into stone, worn as jewelry, and woven into cloth, and are fairly universal in much of Mayan art and culture found up to this day. We do know as well that a priestly class held responsibility for keeping knowledge ñ spiritual and scientific in nature ñ the delineation being far less discrete as is in our time. Mayans considered certain patterns, similar to magic squares, called mats, as sacred. The Mayans designed their mats in many patterns; their craftsmen wove and carved these patterns into stone and cloth. The patterns became known for their specific numbers, power and significance (Daniel Clark Orey, Ph.D. The Mayan Mat: Mathematical Modeling of an Ancient Number Pattern).

Here is more!
8 plus 5 will be 13! My lucky numbers are 85, 58 and 13, 8+5 will be 13. Bad number is 87. 100 minus 13 = 87. Number 13 was extremely important number and

lucky according to the Maya people. For example, Maya 260 days' year was 13 month, with 20 days and each week was 13 days. The universe in the Maya legends had 13 skies![18]

Here is another description of the 5, 8, and 13 according to the Maya culture.
Communicating (5) through time, (Past, Present & Future, (3) becomes the number 8, indicating harmony and balance, and the infinite playing out of duality between all of what exists in the universe and what does not exist except as potential creation. It is my perception that each and every individual consciousness exists at the very center of its own individual Universe. Your consciousness (1) continually communicating (3) with your creation (1) from an established center is 5 plus (8) for infinity creates the number 13.

The Maya had a very clear understanding that all Creation is divided by the number 13. The Mayan priests and kings had a system of time-keeping for each day. A day was equally divided into 13 sections that we would

---

[18] PHI, the "gold ratio" of 1.618, found in many plants and human proportions, in relationship between planets orbiting around our Sun is mathematically derived through the Fibonacci sequence of numbers - 0, 1, 1, 2, 3, **5, 8, 13, 21** and so on. When you divide the larger number by the preceding smaller one, you gradually approach the phi constant. Venus is a very important planet in Maya astrology. As John Martines writes in a LITTLE BOOK of Coincidence: "Venus rotates extremely slowly on her own axis in the opposite direction to most rotations in the solar system. Her day is precisely two-thirds of an Earth year, a musical fifth. This exactly harmonized...so that every time Venus and Earth kiss, Venus does so with the same face looking at the Earth". Eight Earths equals exactly thirteen Venus years, the five kisses between them crafting a perfect pentagon, carved out of space. The numbers 5, 8 and 13 belong to the Gibonacci sequence, defining phi." (Daniel Pinchbeck, 2012 The return of Quetzalcoatl).

call hours. Each section was divided into 13 segments that we would call minutes, which were further divided by 13 to create "seconds." Each second was further divided by 13, and divided again and again to infinity. So, each and every moment experienced by a Mayan was divided infinitely by the number 13.

My daughter was born 21 of July, number 21. Number 21 which is 7, 7, 7, - 3 times and the month is also 7. Now, years later I know that in Chichen Itza the number 7 was a very important number.

Desk or counter top was a representation of all of infinity. Let's make that flat surface stand for the number 8 with the 13 on it. So, if all infinity (8) is consciously divided or individuated out (13) by the Witnessing Creator, this creates the number 21. As described by the Mayan calendar, the number of different aspects of creation equals 20. The number 21 is all of those aspects plus, once again, the Witnessing Creator looking over Its Creation. This number, 21, could be called counting your blessings or gratitude. It could also be seen as a completed step in the ascension of Consciousness. (Ref. 11; Sacred Geometry and the Mayan Calendar, Ian Xel Lungold.
http://www.mayanmajix.com/3nn02_01_04.html)

It is the primary task of Consciousness to become aware of or divide and individuate each and every single particle of creation. You have probably noticed that when you are operating at a relatively heightened level of consciousness, you are able to see the differences between people, objects and events more easily than when your consciousness is operating at a lower frequency, and things look pretty much the same – or even like just one big mess!

b. Everybody has lucky and bad numbers, right?
Yet, in my life, numbers play a mystery role. Maybe it was a daily routine for the Priest, but I never got used to it; on every occasion it still amazed me. Numbers connected with me in some strange way and always advised me of what to do. In my case, if I wish to make an important decision, I ask a question and see what happens. The most extraordinary of these occurrences is when I am on or near a road. I ask the question that needs an answer and instantly cars will start showing up with license plates either with bad or good numbers. Not only that, but they seem to come out of nowhere in great numbers and their license plates always add up to the same number!

Who sent them? How can it be possible that someone knew ahead of time what I would think about at that exact moment? How is it possible for all of the cars to assemble in one place, all at once? And I am not the only one who witnesses this unbelievable event – when it occurs, the people around me could testify to this truly amazing moment. It works in any part of the world.

Here is one of the dreams about numbers. I guess this is how the Priest felt the energy of numbers.

Dream # 9
The power of the four, August 21, 1992

I was lying on a mounted bed. Around me, there was nothing, only space and emptiness. On my right, four creatures started to move away diagonally. Somehow, I had a 360-degree vision. At that moment, on my left side, a crowd of black creatures started approaching, moving sideways (the Roman army moved like that – it's called “a pig”). Everything was black, they were moving straight, all covered in black. First line, there were three, and then the second, and then the leader – number one – in front. They were only waiting. I knew that when the lead-creature would leave, they would tear me apart – into pieces.

I am lying on something like a platform or pedestal – it is my bed; I am not allowed to run away, I am a noble person. I am lying on this bed, in a noble position, like someone self-confident and strong – similar to Buddha. Leaning on my elbows, I "called" the number ones – the leaders. (Not with my voice – I don't have a voice in my dreams). Then they turned and get done with all this quickly.

Now, I understand, what the digit 4 means. In different dimensions, it has different meanings. In one-dimensional space (on a line) they cover the sides, they are of a different color, and then inside the ones – between them – was my place, number 5. Internal distance is filled with a different color. Between them, the connections were very strong and stable (that is why the others were able to scatter). I could see my power. I knew why these four were stronger than the others were.

The four-figure is stronger, than 7 or 9. I don't know why it is very stable. These golden threads through all the space were there again.... When I woke up, I had a strong feeling; these golden threads were spreading, and the body was lying somewhere by itself. It was like a dualization (bifurcation). It was an eternal bliss. I did not feel my body at all. In my dream, when those ones were approaching me... I should not pronounce the words – I am afraid to start worrying, to get irritated. It is dangerous and it pulls me away from the stable, powerful condition in which I live currently. And I never got irritated in my dreams. Irritation brings enormous destruction.

This was the most unusual thing that I saw – before that, I had a flight of spirit, or creativity, or we were somewhere in nature. As a result, at night in my dream, I am rewarded by even larger waves – High Spirit, in a dream, comes to me in stronger waves.

Four is seen as the first solid number; it represents wholeness, totality, completion; a solid foundation. There are four cardinal points; four seasons; four winds; four directions (as in North, South, East, and West); four elements (Fire, Water, Air, Earth) in the western culture. There are four sides to a square; four arms to a cross. There are four rivers in Paradise forming a cross. In the Mayan culture, four giants support the celestial roof. Four is seen as the number of support.

For the Native Americans, as in other cultures, ceremonies and ritual acts are repeated in fours. The Native American cultures have used the number 4 most frequently as in the four cardinal directions. The four winds are depicted by the symbol of the cross and by the symbol of the swastika. Hitler did not create the swastika, as some wrongly believe. It was instead borrowed from the Native American and occult beliefs in which Hitler had great interest. Hitler derived his "insanity" of power from his misdirected interpretation and use of metaphysical principles. He used the knowledge that his human consciousness couldn't possibly understand, and the use of this knowledge for personal gain is part of the imbalance that created the chaos and karma.

In the Egyptian culture, four is the sacred number for the "Time" measurement of the sun. Four pillars support the vault of heaven. There are four canopy jars placed around the dead at the four corners guarded by the four sons of Horus who are associated with the cardinal points. In the Hermetic, it is the divine *quaternity*. It represents God.

Sumero-Semitic: Four astral gods are identified with the four cardinal points.
http://www.crystalinks.com/numerology2.html

8. Plants, agriculture

Plants and agriculture were the main responsibility of the Priest.

I love plants, all of them! I can't live without plants and I spend every single day in the park, walking for close to two hours. This park merges into a wild forest. On my desk, in front of me, right now there are lily-of-the-valley blossoms, lilacs, and three kinds of wild flowers. I spend lots of time in my life studying plants at the university, while taking post-graduate courses. I know how plants live, breathe, grow, feel.

Cut roses can stay in a vase, in good condition, in my home for up to 40 or 45 days! The trick is to keep flowers in non-chlorine water and change the water every three days. Flowers love humidity and it is necessary to spray them with water a few times a day. Trim each stem of their leaves, cut their ends at an angle under the water with a knife, just a little bit every two or three days, and put the bouquet overnight into a bathtub. However, the main ingredient to keep your flowers alive longer is love. I love plants and they feel very good with me. I have some special relationship with them. On the way from the park, five blocks from it, I usually go home just to see how one of my friends, the oak tree, is doing. I hug this tree and say, "How are you?" We have a secret, deep, tender love between us – between me and plants. As soon as I start talking about plants, I radiate with a waterfall of happiness. Anyone who has a good relationship with plants and nature will be healthy, strong, optimistic and full of energy.

I cannot live without plants, period. I remember when I moved to a new city, I lived in an area where there were almost no plants. After two weeks, I felt as if I was "dying" there. I really missed them. It felt almost as if I didn't have enough water or air to survive. I decided to move ASAP. As soon as I moved I was restored and began living in harmony with myself and nature again.

The famous Aristotle said that plants have souls, but do not have feelings (Genady Belimov, "Soul and Intelligence of the Plants", TD 2005).

Today scientists have proved that plants have memory, music ability, consciousness, they even feel people or animals' pain. The American scientist, Cliff Baxter, decided to connect the leaves of a philodendron to a lie detector. The plant showed an instant reaction on paper when suddenly they broke eggs in its proximity. When scientists started boiling shrimps for dinner in the laboratory, each time they dropped a shrimp into boiling water, the plant again showed a reaction indicating sensitivity to the living organism's suffering. When a researcher cut his finger, it was the same, the plant expressed feelings for human pain!

It is a well-known fact that the way to improve an orchard's production is by hitting the trees with the handle of an ax in autumn, and worn them that if they do not give a good harvest the following year they would be cut down! Result: the trees always produce lots of fruits next year!

I read in a magazine about a couple, who was checking their very big garden in autumn, and decided which tree they would cut down in the spring. They marked 35 trees with white chalk. In the spring, they were surprised to see that each tree, which they marked, was dead! None of them had budding leaves on their branches. By the way, ancient people asked a tree for forgiveness before cutting it down.

Another case was even more amazing. It is about an office manager, who loved roses. Each week for years, a bunch of them arrived on his desk. One day he told his staff that he was going on vacation – to the beach. Two days later the flowers were delivered and put on his desk as usual. The roses died almost instantly! The staff couldn't find any reason for this until they went to their boss's home the next day to water his plants and found him dead. He died in his chair with a suitcase nearby, ready to go to the airport. The flowers must have felt that he had a health problem! My advice: try going on vacation when you are still in good health. Don't wait and continue working until you're nearly dead. It is known that plants die within a few hours after their owner died in the same room.

Some orchids can imitate the color of the female insect trying to attract the male insect to pollinate them. In some cases, plants can imitate the smell of rotten meat, trying to attract insects for the same reason. It means plants can see and smell.

During the last century the famous Luter Berbank created many new kinds of plants by talking to them! For example, he talked to a cactus and told it that it would not need needles in its new growing parts because there was no danger in his place; and in case there was looming danger, Luter would protect the cactus. The cactus started growing without needles! In the same manner, Luter Berbank created new kinds of potatoes, fruit trees, flowers, which are now carrying his name. All he did was just to talk to the plants!

Plants react to music; pineapples from Hawaii and Antilles have different taste. The difference was that on Antilles Islands, people sing songs while they are working in the fields!

A garden filled with roses is literally singing, making vibrations, which our ears can't hear, but our spirit, aura can. In Scotland, scientists found that red and black gooseberry prefer Mozart and Giedne music. Strawberry love Brahms and Dvo□ák. Potatoes increase production by listening to Bruckner and Milleara symphonies. It means plants can hear!

Plants can even read people's thoughts. Scientists have put that theory to the test by thinking positively and wishing the plants good health. These plants showed excellent reactions to "positive thinking" and grew healthy, and happy! Production increased up to 30% with potatoes, for example. The opposite is also true; when a negative person lives around plants, the negativity seems to stem their growth.

As you can see I can talk about plants forever...

I was studying the famous Vavilov's wild wheat collection, which he collected from all over the world for future selection. During the Second World War, in Leningrad, thousands of people died from hunger, but no one took any grain from this rare collection – not a single seed. They preserved it for the benefit of future generations. What a strong spirit these people had! Now all over the world, those priceless seeds have produced new generations of wheat, growing and feeding millions of people!

Dream # 10
The Great Harmony of Nature

That evening, I knew that I would have a dream ... Something special.

I saw some two or three kinds of "men" (not human) – more like some "guides". Maybe they were the spirits of people. I seem to be reporting to them. You and me – we are reporting to these "guides". It was some kind of "valley", by that I mean there is nothing there.... It's as if this valley is covered by fog. I seem to be walking "in" a cloud – only to my waist. And that is all, there is nothing more; not on top not at the bottom. The fog is like vapor, steamy – something monotonous, no landscape. We are together with you in this valley, and you were helping me, we had to find maybe six or ten plants that I had planted there. We were looking for them, were picking them and had to show them to those "spirit-ones" as if it were some sort of a test. They were somehow strange flowers, like a big flower on a pedicle. I remember one of them close to me. When I took it to put together with the others, I made an adjustment to it. And when I looked at it closely, it was a sphere – a divided sphere (I repeated it to myself later, it was important) 20 centimeters in diameter. They had a white background with lilac diagonal lines crisscrossing them. I moved my finger on one of them and made the diagonals longer. These diagonals divided the sphere in 12 sections, like an astrology chart. After I lengthened these diagonals, we carried the spheres to those creatures. It seems to me, that there was also a woman there, a female spirit, like an angel, very light. Then suddenly, when I carried all this to them, I turned around and looked back, and the entire place was covered with emerald leaves. It looked like a rice field I saw in Japan. They all were covered with large beads of dew – as big as grapes. The beads of dew attracted my attention. I saw, that on the side, on the edge, the valley was surrounded by vertical rocks. Clear, fresh water came out from these rocks – waterfalls. The water was purified as it passed through the rocks.

Afterwards something unusual, beautiful started to happen... Water, rocks – all this was tentative, not real, and the grass as well... Those were symbols. It was like the fog was taking different shapes and qualities in different places ... And all this started to talk to me... (I got goose bumps all over my skin). It was tremendous, astonishing law... Nature itself was telling me its law, but "law" is a very strong word.... Nature was telling about its ... way of living ... how they all are existing in harmony ... and their energy in such harmony, all in brilliance. At the same time, I felt the soft, warm energy of the sun.... Everything is so transparent, clear, harmonious ... It was telling me all this step by step ...And when in one moment it seemed to me that something was missing, they told me more, and it turned out to be the key to all that was said before.... Something from the humans, something very fine and fragile, indistinguishable, very harmoniously flowed into it.... All this is one life.... And I thought that I should write a book about it. And then I looked and saw in front of me a large book, and one page is written – dedicated to what I was told, and already clearly, and explicitly written, as if by myself.... Curly letters, very-very beautiful calligraphy. I started reading it.... I remember that it was a dream, and I had to remember it well. I tried to find human words and even tried to remember the order of words. Step after step. It was hard work, very strange. After all these efforts, I woke up.

What is most interesting, when I woke up and got out of this condition, a part of me was bigger than the ones that live here. The large one was from somewhere above, from far away. It was watching when I, the little one, was coming back. It was like the sun and one ray coming from it.... In what condition of life am I coming back this time? It was a very strong and very real sensation. And so this sun, the main part, saw my life with its own eyes – that is, I saw it with her eyes – that I am returning to such a warm, cozy, soft untroubled spot; something like a nest, something calm, like a pool or a lake. There was neither satisfaction, nor anything else from the one, BIG part of me that I was here, only a very clear, cold observation....

Then, I woke up. I was lying on my back, trying to remember who I am, and how I fell asleep.... It seemed to me, that the BIG side of me told me that a human being could exist without food, while being in harmony with nature. He told me specifically not to eat animals. There was energy of water, energy of rocks, and energy of plants. They were not real plants, rocks, water – this was all clearly symbolic. The water was extraordinary. There were no animals, birds, fish, or insects. There was something very fine, something of a human sort, very specific – and we especially should not eat them. The humans should not eat at all! If a person is placed in this harmony, s/he does not need feeding.

Dream # 11
Luminous Bodies of Plants, January 8, 1992

I hadn't slept all night. Again, like the other times, I was dreaming of unusual things within five minutes of my being asleep. I can remember it, because I woke up right after that. It was maybe 5:00am. I was lying in bed. At this moment a terrible sound, a terrible click made me open my eyes – as if some shot went off in my room. I remembered my dream – and at the same moment, there was this shot, a terrible sound, like dry wood cracking. I jumped, opened my eyes, and I could still hear the shot. Something like that used to happen with my piano. I fell back to sleep and again something unusual came to my dreams. Again, this shot, and I woke up again. Very strong sound.

I was dreaming that I approached the window, there was some space in front of me, and different kinds of trees had been planted in rows. There were some apple trees, pines, birch-trees, a whole variety, and rare breeds as well. I looked at them. In my mind, I knew what kind of trees they were, but with my eyes, I saw them in colors. I was shocked – I hadn't seen this before. The trees of the same breed were of the same color. They had approximately three spectra. I remembered what apple trees looked like, their color was orange; what the fir trees looked like – they consisted of three lines of the spectrum, I think, bright blue. If the blue is responsible for dynamic of growth, it should be on the top, where the new growth is. But it turned out to be not so, the fir tree had it in the middle, 2/3 from the bottom – a blue line, then bright-yellow, and perhaps a red one. I don't remember now, I cannot remember clearly. The apple tree had a soft orange tone, coming into rose, but two separate colors, like on those balloons.

You opened a book and started reading – a prologue. You were reading aloud with my voice. At the same time, the other me, was observing the scene from outside. I interrupted your reading. I knew what was written there, right away, although I heard it for the first time. In this book, the knowledge came to the surface, which was unknown to people until then. This book was a revelation. People did not even suspect it – it opened up, revealing itself like an old secret, a treasure, as if someone dug it out of the earth. A very rare animal, a diamond animal was buried there thousands and thousands of years ago. I interrupted myself and started dictating the already specific things from this book (you had only the introduction). You started to write down what I was saying immediately.

Dream # 12
Spectrum, February 23, 1992

Many trees, large clearing, they were growing not one by one, but as if united for some purpose. I thought – well, what a clearing, and I saw it in my dream for the first time. However, I knew that it is not a dream, but a reality. After that, some living creature appeared in the clearing – either a dog, or a person, I don't remember now. And it was also consisting of those spectrums. It was going on for so long, that I could look for as long as I wanted, at all of the details, transformations of colors, and I divided all this into a system. I counted how many breeds of trees there were, how many colors, everything. It was very unusual, beautiful, and at the same time more real than the trees ever were.
Incredible!

9. Masks.

The priest always had his mask with him.

I always wished to have a mask, but the type I needed, I could never find in any store. I wished to have a full size mask, covering my entire face. Now I am wearing one – it is a jaguar mask; it makes me very comfortable and happy. It is always in front of my eyes, on the wall or on my head.... My business partner in London wished to give me something as a souvenir, and he was very surprised when I asked him to find a jaguar mask for me.

10. Caracol - the name of the observatory in Chichen Itza.

The town of Caracol is near Tibet where my parents were born and where I grew up. It seems as if Spirit before I was born searched for a place with a similar name. It is interesting that in 1987, I saw the name Caracola on the map of Turkmenistan and I was attracted to this place like a magnet. I felt as if someone called me to come. Caracola is like a quad – a meeting place. I flew there. I went through the Time Gate to the many dimensional worlds and I had an astonishing contact there. Guess what? It was a meeting with my own Spirit from the future in a new body! You can see in another chapter, KUKULCAN, a drawing from this "spirit". This place is close to the place where the Spirits, creatures from my dreams contact me from time to time. (You name them if you can. It is not easy for me to find words to describe them or give them a name, because some of them are different from our world and I don't have anything to compare them with.)

11. Aztec God Xochipilli

For many years, I often held a little wooden man in my hands. It was a gift, which was carved for me by a handsome boy, soon after we met. I inspired him to make this little wooden man. After many years, a week ago, I found that this little statue is the Aztec God, Xochipilli, the God of flowers, corn, and love. He plays with a ball; he loves beauty, songs, dances and fun! He usually sits between flowers and butterflies with a sharp stiletto in his hand, on the end of which there is a human heart!

12. I always want to be Priest – during my present life!

My best friend is a High Priest from Asia.

Three years ago, I was living in Asia in a Buddhist temple. I loved harmony, meditation, nature and the wise Buddhist philosophy they taught there. In this ancient, beautiful temple, every evening the monks play huge drums, the size of a wall, maybe 2.5 to 3 meters in diameter. Instead of drumsticks, they use the trunk of a tree! The magnificent sound they produce comes out in waves of strong, powerful vibrations, which flows far away to the valley and mountains around. On the opposite side, in front of the main temple, the monks play on big gongs and on a few drums. I am sure these monks are the best drummers in the world. You know why? Each of our moves is an impulse from the brain connected through the nervous system. The monks' brains are extremely organized due to the many hours of daily meditation, which last sometimes for weeks, so all of this energy moves through the channels smoothly, without friction, onto their drums. A few years ago, I read an article about some research done in San Diego about the brain of the Buddhist monks. The scientists found that the monks' portion of their brains dedicated to pleasure and happiness is 25% larger! Wow! They must be the happiest people on the planet.

Every evening the monks play huge drums...

They enjoy life much more than we do. I think this is the reason for the light of happiness and kindness, which shines from their eyes.

There were 250 Buddhist monks, men and women living in the Temple. They have a big kitchen where monks and guests share their meals. One day I was sitting near two monks. I heard one telling the other; "Today, in my dream, I will travel to . . . galaxy," naming the exact galaxy where he intended to journey during his dream. Then the second monk replied, "I will join you." To this, their teacher, the head of the monastery, who was sitting nearby, said, "I will follow you both, and I will check on you today." Apparently, this is part of their daily routine. I was very envious! All they do is sleep and meditate...! Afterwards they talk for hours about there dreams....

I even asked the top monk to accept me as a monk into this temple and he asked me if I was ready to cut all my long, golden hair. I cut 70 cm that summer, and still had another 50 cm on my head. That was not a problem for me, since my hair grows very fast as if I were a "wild animal", with lots of thick, long hair, down to my hips. The Priest told me that this is a sign of strong energy. I always receive many compliments about my hair. However, when I was modeling my agent asked me to cut my hair many times, because women just do not have such strong, long hair when they are in their thirties. I remember ending up buying a short wig to try to hide my hair under it! It was funny![19]

I discovered during my studies that each little hair is a long tube, inside which there is a channel filled with electro conductivity mass. On the cover of the hair, charges are besieged with a thin coat of what we call PRANA energy. Women with long hair bring energy to the fetus during pregnancy. The short hair fashion, which women have right now, cuts the possibility for the fetus to receive necessary PRANA for its development. This is why so many kids are born unhealthy or weak. Some women may also experience problems during childbirth and with lactation. In many cultures, cutting a woman's hair was prohibited during pregnancy. Doctors also noticed that women's hair starts to be fuller, thicker during pregnancy. As a result – of following a fashion trend or a cultural tradition – people, from one generation to another, have degenerative health.

---

[19] It is interesting that in my past lives as a Priest, a woman from Atlantis, a girl from Egypt – everyone had very long, thick hair. Except Amelia, who had good, long hair when she was young, but cut short later, which was suitable for her woman-pilot image, and which was in fashion at that time. A Honorable Supreme Buddhist monk told me that one of my past lives was in this temple as a High Buddhist monk. It looks like this is what attracted me always to the Buddhist part of Asia: Japan, South Korea and China.

While I was living in that temple, the monks asked me about my dreams: what I saw, where I went, how many times I had been in the same places and how many times I saw the same dreams – in as many details as I could. This analysis gave them an idea as to the amount and level of special spiritual energy I have, and about the stage of my spirit development. They complimented me many times about my energy, and as a result, I got a Blessing from the Honorable Supreme Buddhist monk, who is the leader of 13 million monks in Asia. We developed a very good friendship between him and me.

As for me, he is the wisest man on the planet. Each of his words and sentences is filled with deep spiritual meaning. Some special, heavenly, beautiful, white, glowing energy fills the space and the whole room around him. After talking to him, when you go outside, it feels as if you are returning from Heaven – from the sky down to Earth's reality. To me, he is a "Live Buddha" here on the planet.

"Live Buddha"

He drew something for me – a gift – a painting with hieroglyphs, which meant “One of a kind”.

I asked him, “Why?” He told me that I am very rare, because of some special qualities my Spirit has. As for me, I think that every human is *one of a kind* and this belongs to the same kind of idea. Remember Mr. Alfons: “I am who I am, I am not more then somebody else, I am not less then somebody else. I am myself.” I am one of a kind here on Earth. Period.

I don’t belong to any religion; there was a time in my life when I was searching for it. That until I saw in a dream a special place – I called this place White Emptiness. I returned to this dream from time to time, and this glowing white, pure energy place, which is absolutely empty – nothing around, nothing under or on top – is the most sacred place for me, because, this place gives me the most amazing, beautiful feeling I ever had in my whole life. If there were ever a new religion based on White Emptiness, I would be the first person to sign up – waiting near the door or on the stairs. The monks also know about this place and they asked me to give them every detail about my travels there. What could I say? What details?

There is NOTHING there, right…? My advice to you is to start meditating, and you might discover the door leading to this new world, bright and beautiful like a “sky full of stars and galaxy in eternity”.

13. Tortoise

I like turtles a lot! I have a collection of them. From a young age, until now, I always have a live one near me, a little one, around 5 to 6 cm in diameter. When I didn’t have a little turtle during my first few years in Canada, I often had many dreams where I tried to find my tortoise. Then I called Tibet asking them to find the smallest one in the desert and to send it to me. As soon as I got it, everything went back into harmony. My little turtle usually loves to sleep on my desk under the cozy, green lamp, while I am typing. It looks like a little, shiny rock down there. In this Buddhist temple, there were tortoises everywhere, carved in wood and rocks, but not a real, live one in sight. So I gave a little live-turtle to my friend for his 80th birthday.

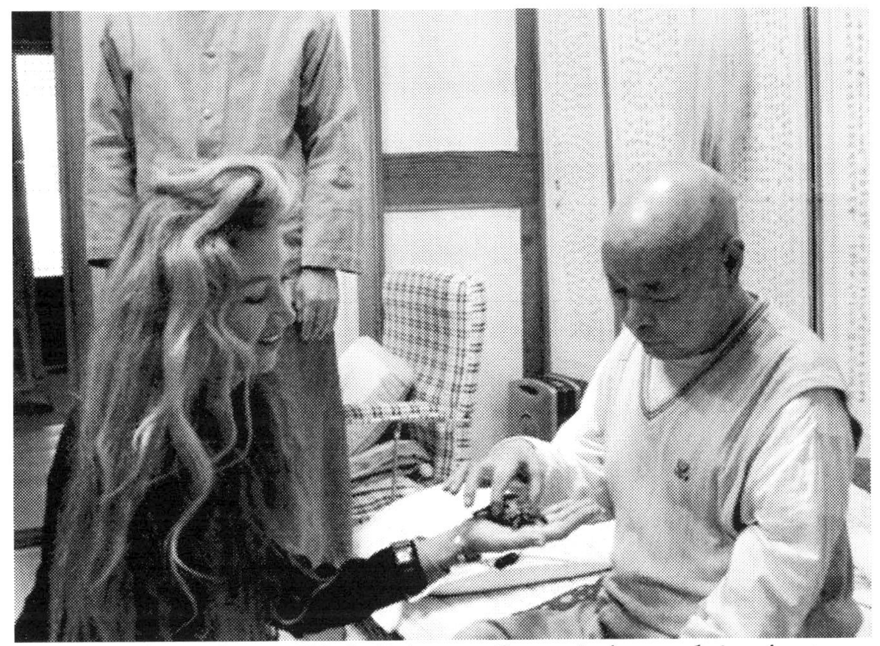

Meeting of two High Priests: from Asia and Ancient Mexico, turtle gift exchange.

I always travel with my turtle. This is the main reason I always have very small size ones. Once, I was at the Frankfurt airport going through customs. When it came time for me to go through the checkpoint, I was asked to put everything through the X-ray. Since I didn't want my turtle to be subjected to radiation, I kept her in my pocket. The officers then asked, “What do you have in your pocket?” I told them it was a toy.

Next, they asked me, “Why is your toy moving?” I was traveling, as usual, in my silky jaguar cape and no one would imagine that I had a live turtle in my pocket – however, this time it looked like my tortoise woke up and was making a fuss. I pulled my little pet out. Everyone around me then started screaming and yelling for assistance. Yet, since I have all the documents necessary to go through any border – veterinarian passport, etc. – and a little cage for her, there was no problem. We all ended up laughing.

14. Connection with the Goddess Bodhisattva, meeting with God.

Goddess Bodhisattva

In this old, ancient Buddhist temple, there is a 1,500-year-old legend.

The monks found this place, high in the mountains. There was a very special, pure energy about the place and they started dreaming of building a temple there. However, they didn’t have money to erect the temple. They prayed for many months for somebody to help them realizing their dream. One day, a girl came and told them that she would work and help them in the kitchen. She was a magnificent, beautiful creature! Soon people started to come from the villages around, just to see her beauty and began donating money for the temple. More and more people came every day. One day, a rich man arrived with his son and gave the money necessary to build the temple. His son, on the other hand, fell in love with this girl. The wedding and the Temple’s inauguration were scheduled for the same day. Many people gathered for the celebration. At the moment, when everyone stood in front of the temple and the wedding ceremony was about to start, the girl suddenly decided to change something in her outfit. She ran straight into a huge rock near the temple and disappeared in front of hundreds of people! In the middle of this rock her little sock got stuck. Since then, every year one flower blossoms in the place where she lost her sock.

The monks believe that she was Goddess Bodhisattva – the best among all Gods and Goddesses when it comes to serve people's needs and help them in their pursuits. This is why, on the statues, sometimes she is represented with many hands to help everyone. From time to time, she visits Earth as a human. The monks invited me to visit the huge rock where she disappeared. I wore my golden outfit for this ceremony. They told me that if I would tell her name three times and ask for something, it would happen. I did it all according to their rituals; I stayed on my knees on this marble floor in front of her statue and began to concentrate. Suddenly, I saw Goddess Bodhisattva standing on a big turtle!

Wow! When I saw this, I felt an instant connection with her, as if she was my friend and we knew each other forever, and we have the same interests – she loves tortoises! Then I started calling her, by repeating her name: "Kwansaeum Bosal, Kwansaeum Bosal, Kwansaeum Bosal." Next, I told her in one sentence: "Please make me successful in my business, so I will be able to help this temple."

Suddenly, the air around me began to feel very hot! I found myself in the middle of an enormous flame and it sparkled! I experienced heavenly, beautiful energy around me. I enjoyed being in this sparkling cloud,

which wrapped around my body like a cocoon. It continued to surround me for 2 to 3 minutes.
The monks, who had stayed near me, saw it; felt it and they were in total shock! They decided that this was a sign that maybe I am the Goddess Bodhisattva and that I had come to visit the temple again..., and they reported what happened to the top monk.

As for me, I don't know how to explain this. It is evident that she came and was around me.... The monks asked me what I did. I told them that I started calling for her to come to me. Perhaps I didn't understand the translation that I should just pronounce her name and say my wish. Maybe it was the Spirit of the Maya Priest which is inside me who intervened. He used to be in connection with God and he would know exactly how to deal with Goddesses.

During the next three weeks, the monks brought me the best Korean pears and some of the fruits, which are usually given to the three Gold Buddha statues in the main temple. Most importantly, though, I got a blessing and special prayers in the temple on my birthday and I was showered with Buddhist presents! It was a happy time!

Meeting with God

It was Christmas Morning.

Red carnations and white chrysanthemums filled the biggest Catholic Church in Vancouver and it was packed with people. The priest was talking and talking... but as for me, I didn't feel any energy, I didn't feel any life in it... His speech was empty....

What kind of message is he sending to people on this special day? I guess he just tried, but he must not have had enough sleep after the midnight service. Suddenly he decided to ask people to say something special.... I was right! He needed help today. I got up and found myself talking to 300-400 people on Christmas day. I told them:

"It was the day when I should have given birth to my baby. I did not sleep all night except for a few minutes. I had a dream, but everything in this dream was very real! *Two angels arrived, two real angels with white wings*! I remember flying with them and they guided me from both sides. They brought me to the church on the hill.... A tall priest came to me from this church with the parishioners following him.... He stopped in front of me and he blessed me... I saw his face... I recognized him instantly!" (As I am typing these lines, I am covered with goose bumps again....)

"I woke up at 8:00am and the contractions started.... Exactly 24 hours later, I gave birth to a healthy baby girl."

The next part of my dream, I did not tell the people in church but I will relate it to you now. When intellectual people who do not believe in astrology, and especially those who visit the Catholic Church – if I were to tell them this part, they would start thinking that I am crazy and they would lose interest in the priceless gold dime in this story. Doctors were worried about the baby and me. The problem was that I turned my body clock to give birth to my baby three weeks later in order for her to have a perfect astrology chart on the day she was born. I had locked the door for the baby to come out into the world. I just needed one more day.... I went through all of the stages of labor and imminent delivery, but the situation was still the same and the doctors could do nothing about it. I ended up having a C-section. After the birth, they called me a hero and told me that I went through all possible and impossible phases of birthing and they thought I would die. All the while, I felt Him nearby, He held my hand....

YES, I told all these people in the church that, "I grew up in a country where people were atheist, no one went to church for 75 years. Until that day, when I had this dream, I never thought about GOD, I never visited a church. Since it happened, I know that GOD exists. Angels exist. And they take care of each and everyone of us. I then began to respect people who never met GOD during their lifetime or in their dreams, BUT believe that He exists and have His Holy Faith in their hearts!"

People liked my story; some of them ran after the service to talk to me. I like this church, especially for the beautiful cut-glass windows, with scenes portraying God's life, and for the wonderful organ music.

Here is the exact dream with all of the details, for those who are interested.

Dream # 13
God's Blessing, angels, July 20, 1995

There were two dreams. I remembered only one. I slept from 5:00 to 8:00. It was at the time, when I was expecting a baby. I had a dream, but everything in this dream was very real! Two little children appeared beside me – small, up to my knees, but they understood everything, as if they were not five years old, but much older. They started pulling me on both sides – as if I should go with them somewhere; they should bring me to some place. *It was two real angels with white wings!* They took me and I remember flying with them and they guided me from both sides. I started moving, and they stayed with me, floating in the air, not touching the ground but floating beside me at my waist. They brought me to the church, the cathedral on the hill. Near this cathedral, I saw a priest surrounded by other people. He saw me and immediately came to meet me, as if he was expecting me.

He was very tall, very thin, very strict in his manner and clean. Young – as if he was 33 years old, but wise, as if he were thousands of years old – not a person, but a Saint. I looked around. The cathedral was snow-white, very severe. I looked up. It had one cupola, but it went very high up, in eternity. It was shining – snow-white, clear and high. I don't know with what to compare it – some mountains are like that, crystal-clear, untouched, virginal.

He approached me and started saying something. I knew that it was some kind of ritual, an important ritual. There was a feeling, that this day was a day of sacral feast. I was wearing something; I put it on to go to the hospital – what I wore before falling asleep. He made some movements around me with his arms and something, a cover, shiny as snowflakes came down on me from above. When it fell down on me – my shoulders and my back were covered with soft white fur, like swans' feathers, very fine.

Then he made a roundish move in the air with his arms, as if making a circle downright, and completed it as if by drawing a line under my breast. And I understood that women's breast is a symbol of maternity, and not something else. My breast swelled. It was filled with a sensation of elasticity. Then he made a gesture with his hand, with a finger – some sign in front of me – he raised the forefinger of the right hand and moved it to the side. I turned around and looked behind me, to the north-west, I think (I felt goose bumps in my dream) – and there were hundreds and hundreds of people standing in a form of a triangle. They all looked at me silently, as if waiting, as if I had a mission, and it was my high responsibility. I felt uneasy. Seriously. They were different people. I remembered only the people in front – they were old, old wise men, wearing different clothes, of different epochs, like in a museum of history. There was boyar, another in a sable coat, the third one in something else.... I understood – this was my clan, and I am on the edge of the clan. I turned to the priest and I suddenly understood what he was doing – he was blessing me. I just had enough time to tell him, that I liked very, very much his cathedral, of eternal beauty, splendid, clear, white... I opened my eyes – it was eight o'clock. And my first contraction started....

As for me, I think God exists and He is the only one. However, through human eyes he can be perceived in a variety of shapes and forms, depending on the religion and beliefs of each person.

Something very odd happened to me in Rome, at the Vatican, in the summer of 2008. We went with my daughter through St. Peter's Basilica with crowds of tourists and we needed to rush back to the tour bus. While we were inside, I saw, not far from the exit, a statue with two baby angels, exactly the same size and looks as what I saw in my dream! I asked my daughter to take a photo and I asked her to take a few photos outside.

When we went outside, I decided to cross the square. As soon as I was alone and somewhat separated from people, I instantly felt the very strong presence of someone near me! My whole body was covered with goose bumps ... and I started talking to this Spirit. I told him that I felt him and so on, and so on.... My daughter didn't notice it! Since we were very rushed, she ran ahead and turned to take some pictures while I was totally in shock with this astounding feeling of talking to this Spirit! In the middle of a sunshiny day! And with thousands of people around!

Julia agape in front of St. Peter's Basilica

At first, I stopped agape, as if the ground in front of me suddenly opened and there was no place for me to take the next step. Afterwards, I talked to this Spirit as if he were a long lost friend.... Wow! I have no idea who he was....

I remember, when I stopped I was not worrying about our bus anymore; I just looked around me as if in a daze. When I turned around, I saw Jesus holding a cross in his hand and with his apostles surrounding him. Surrounding the square in front of the St. Peter's Basilica, there are many statues of "Holy" people, they are very special to the Catholic faithful, and the Church pronounced them "Holy" or canonized them. Perhaps it was a "Holy" man who guided me through my dreams. Or maybe it was the spirit of Michelangelo who came to me in front of St. Peter's Basilica? He invested his creativity and an enormous amount of energy everywhere around this place, into the paintings and the statues. Maybe Michelangelo wanted to *thank me* for dedicating this book to him and other creative people? Or maybe it was Jesus? It is possible – since this place resounded of such a strong energy. Maybe right there, in another dimension, which is invisible to us, this is the church where the real GOD, Jesus exists and where I was invited, guided by two little angels, and blessed by God right before my baby was born?

It is interesting that since it happened, as soon as I started remembering that moment, I experienced again the same sensation: my body was covered with goose bumps. It means that the Spirit knew I was thinking about him at that exact moment – and it's happening again right now, while I am typing these words....

Julia in front of Jesus in the Church of the Holy Wisdom, known as Hagia Sophia, Istanbul

The scientist who led the team responsible for cracking the human genome says he has found GOD. Francis Collins, the director of the US National Human Genome Research Institute, has written a new book: "The Language of God," arguing that there is nothing in science that contradicts the existence of God. On the contrary, Collins says his research has convinced him that God is real!

In this book, the pioneering geneticist argues that, "Today we are learning the language in which God created life". He believed that sequencing of the human genome is in fact the most remarkable of the texts, offering a detailed view of the mind of the creator at work.

"Science is not threatened by God. It is enhanced" and "God is most certainly not threatened by science. He made it all possible." In staking out a position in support of the existence of God, Collins joins some of the history's most influential scientists – Isaac Newton, and Albert Einstein, *(Magazine, "Atlantis Rising", number 59, "Genome pioneer discovers God").*

15. Ghosts

When people die, their Spirit goes to Heaven. However, some are stuck in between for different reasons: some are attached to the house, where they live, or to a real person, or things they had in this life... Some worry that God will not accept them because they were not baptized or did something wrong in this life, and some don't know that they are actually dead. God will accept everyone. People should go directly to the white glowing light. Simple – and they will be taken care of. People who die and Spirit in heaven show up to me usually very nicely, beautiful, in the best shape they had during their lives. Ghost are instead not here and not there, they are stuck in the space between Heaven and Earth and show up ugly, deformed, partly decomposed even... yak!

It is easy for a ghost to appear in a humid climate. I lived in Tokyo many times, always for a few months. I remember the first time I went to Japan; I arrived at this building from the airport very tired and went to sleep instantly. Someone, during the night, touched me and patted me lightly on the back, without stopping – no break, no rest – and he laughed all night long into my ears! It was exhausting. I remember ending up screaming, "Go away! Go away! Stop it! Stop it! Stop it!" I asked this "someone" to go away all night long! When I woke up in the morning, I told my friend, Lisa, about it. She replied, "This is our ghost; it bothers everyone in this building!"

I asked her, "What you mean ghost?"

She said, "Look out the window." Near the building was a huge cemetery! She told me that everyone in the building knew about ghosts and there was not a thing they could do about it. This building, with its adjoining cemetery, was located in the middle of modern Tokyo, near the TV station.

I returned to my apartment in the same building at around 7:30 p.m. My mother, who was a doctor, from an early age taught me to wash my hands as soon as I returned home. Seeing that the light was on in the washroom, I thought someone was in there. A few minutes later, I called, "Anyone home?" No answer. I then decided to put the kettle on the stove to make some tea and waited for a few seconds. At the same moment, a drawer and a door from the kitchen cabinets popped open loudly! The drawer on top contained spoons, forks, knifes; the cupboard below stored big things like pots. In order to open it, someone should have pulled the first drawer near the wall, and the other door needed to be pulled from inside, where I stood in amazement.

I returned to my seat at the kitchen table and began thinking about this like a scientist. "How can it be possible? I just put the teakettle on the stove and it didn't start boiling yet. It would be impossible for the difference in temperature to create this." I really didn't have any explanation. I then looked at the bathroom door. Still no sign of anyone being in there. I pulled on the door; it did not open. I started calling, "Someone inside?" No reply. I pulled on the door harder and opened it. No one inside! It was empty!

My first thought was, "What silly girls live here," because the entire floor was covered with unrolled toilet paper.... Next, I was amazed! Really amazed! Someone inside had taken the toilet paper from the roll, which was located near the door, dragged it along the wall and wrapped it many times around the towel bar, on the door, until the roll was empty. There had been many layers wrapped around the towel bar, and when I had pulled the door hard, the ball of wrapped paper had ripped in the middle and had unraveled itself across the floor!

"How can this be possible?" – That question came back to mind immediately. There is only one way for someone to unravel an entire roll of toilet paper and roll it around the doorknob – with time and very patiently. Secondly, what really hit me: someone did it from inside, but there was no one, nobody inside! Our apartment was located on the fourth floor and there was NO window – no access to the washroom except through the door. How this can be possible?

I was totally lost with two unexplained events. Then I remembered the previous night's disturbance and Lisa's comments about the ghosts in this building.

The Priest

Lucky for me Lisa returned home soon and told me that many strange things happened in this apartment. She told me that sometimes the curtains blew up in front of her and blankets were ripped off her bed, or someone had scratched her hand while she was eating....

The second night I did not sleep again. Again, someone try to "play" with me all night long. I began remembering that in Russia people from far away villages called this sort of spirit "chekotilki" – those who tickle people to death.

However, an even more horrible thing happened close to the morning. In my dream, I saw my friend, the famous opera singer, Slava. Slava had a voice, which could heal people. When friends came to see him, he always asked the person to stay in front of him while he adjusted their energy. Sometimes during this procedure, people started to levitate and ended up only being supported by their toes. After this procedure, people felt like they were newborn babies, full of energy and harmony. In the dream, I did what he asked and my feet started lifting. Suddenly something horrible happened! Something came inside me from under my feet, went through my body, up to my chest and stayed there – some sort of enormous pressure, like a two-ton-truck had settled against my chest and was compressing my lungs. I couldn't breathe. I saw my mother, she was calling my father, she was screaming for help! The pressure was finally released with a terrible blow and it left me with the most awful pain in my lungs. I woke up and I could hardly breathe! Each breath was painful for me. This ghost pretended to be my friend and I trusted him. This allowed him to do these horrible things!

That day I called Canada but I couldn't really talk – my voice was but a whisper. People asked why I talked like that. I tried to tell them that a ghost had come during my dream and had settled on my body. They didn't believe me; instead they told me to "get some sleep!"

"I wish I could," I said, "but it's impossible." When I told them that I could not sleep because of some ghost, they started worrying about my mental health...

It was already the third night since I left Canada and I had not slept a wink in four days. I was sick and tired of that damn ghost! I was even thinking about people who die because of lack of sleep. My neighbors told me that many people had moved from this building because of the ghosts. Some of them tried to sleep during the day. In my condition, in my deeply tired state of mind, it was impossible for me to start looking for another apartment in a country where I arrived only three days ago.

I returned home the next day, no one was there. After the previous night's events I was afraid to fall asleep. I understood clearly that even if someone is not alone in the apartment, while you are sleeping, in your dream you are still alone – one on one with the ghost!

I went to the neighbors, the girls who lived on the seventh floor. Only one was there and she told me that my friend and her roommate went to a party at Hero Park! "They'll return maybe in the morning!" she said. I spent the whole night reading magazines at her place. She told me that what happened with my lungs happened also, in exactly the same way, to one girl living with her. It took three weeks for her to return back to normal.

At 6 a.m. the girls returned and I finally went back to the 4th floor to my home. It was twilight already when I lay down on my bed. As soon as I closed my eyes, I saw a Japanese girl standing near my bed! I sat up and looked at her. She looked at me in total silence. No emotions, nothing. I only remember that I thought, "What a sick girl!"

I woke up... I am not sure that I even went to sleep at all... and I went to my roommates. The two of them, and one from the 7th floor, were sitting in the living room next to the open door to my room, eating. I asked them, "Who is this Japanese girl? Why has she come to visit us so early? Is she our neighbor? I need rest!" They looked at me and replied, "You went to sleep ten minutes ago, when we were already eating right here, no one came in. No one went to your room. The only way to go to your room from the entrance door is through the living room where we are all eating right now."

They were right – the only other way to my room was from the balcony – on the 4th floor. I told them, "This is impossible! I saw her right here, a minute ago! I remember her in all the little details!"

"Okay! Tell us what she looks like."

I described her. She was 25 or 26 years old maybe, a modern girl, but her face was very pale, ashen. Usually, Japanese girls have very nice white face. But this one seemed very sick; she had dark, really dark, black circles under her eyes and cheeks.

One of the girls told me, "You describe someone from the "Adams family!"" It was obvious to everyone that a ghost was visiting us – no one else.... Again, the word "obvious" sounds strange when talking about ghosts.

I was fed up! I needed rest. It was the fourth morning after another sleepless night. That day I decided to go to the cemetery. No two ways about it, I wanted to talk to these ghosts and stop this harassment! Especially, I wished to talk to that Japanese girl. I know that it was her who was playing during the night trying to attract my attention. And I wanted to talk to those who “sat” on my lungs!

I hate ghosts, you never know what to expect from them. They’re kind of sticky, grand masters at creating fear and existing on it. They’re very creative in the way they trick people. They are lost souls . . . nothing to add.

I invited the girls to go with me to the cemetery, but they were afraid to death! (Pardon the pun.) No one wanted to go. I told them that in their dreams they were on their own with this ghost and I could not help them if that were to happen. The goal was to let the ghosts know that we were aware of them, that we were not going to pay attention to them, that we would have no part of their games and that we would not support them or feed them with our fearful energy – so that they would have to leave us alone.

So here I am. I left Canada four days ago and now I am in a Tokyo cemetery talking to ghosts!

I was wearing my beautiful red sari, a silk dress from Nepal, maybe five meters long if you opened it. I lit a candle, and started calling the ghosts to come to the meeting by knocking on the little wooden monk bells from China. And I started talking to them with my full voice. It was almost dark now. I told them that I came here to Japan for a modeling job and that I was here because I did not sleep for four days, that I was sick and tired of them and that I couldn’t take it anymore! “It needs to stop!” I hollered.

Julia talking to ghosts in the Japanese cemetery

I just started the preparation to wear a sari and flowers on my head, and I put my camera on some tomb, up high – set on "automatic" – to make this photo. But it was dark already, I had a hard time setting up the timer, and I was too tired to do it a second time, so I have only one photo. The photo is AS IS before I was ready to start. The reason for my trying to take a photo; I was hoping to see maybe a sign of the ghosts on the film... I guess I should have asked one of the ghosts to press the button on the camera!

I told them again that I needed rest to look good for my work. I repeated that they should stop their tricks, never come to me again, and never bother me! I said that I didn't want to hear them, feel them and know about them. Period. I told them that all of them were dead and their place was in heaven . . . instead of being stuck here and creating problems for all the people in this building. I also said that they should feel really ashamed of what they were doing.

It was starting to get really dark now – no light – except for the light from a window on the second floor of the building. Suddenly I saw a bunch of them standing near me – they were surrounding me! Perhaps more than ten kind of white people's shadows! Like pieces of fog... To my surprise, instead of being scared, I was glad that I made my speech in "public", not to the empty air. I told them, "I see that you all were listening to me carefully. Very good! BYE forever," and I returned home.

And you know what? They never, ever bothered me again. They never came to me! When my friend slept during the day or I woke up early, I saw that she tossed and turned all the time in her bed, in her room – as if someone was pinching her without stopping....

****

Hold on! The fire alarm just came on – on our floor – it's ringing right now!

"Bye for now... I need to run and see if the house is on fire..." My daughter is already in the hallway with our ferret in her arms....

I am back; it was the fire alarm on our floor alright. Our neighbor ran for the manager. He checked everything and told us that he doesn't have any idea why it was ringing.... I am suspicious that this Japanese girl showed up. Really! Because at the moment it started ringing I decided to be done with the ghosts and said, "Bye for now" to the Japanese girl!

When I am reading now the last sentence I wrote before the fire alarm started ringing..., "They never, ever bothered me again. They never came to me!" Wow! I know why the fire alarm started ringing! The Japanese girl – right! She doesn't bother me in my dreams now, but I was connected to her for a long time. Okay, I will tell you the full story about my "friendship" with ghosts.

****

The next day I talked to the priest at the cemetery and asked him about the Japanese girl. He told me that, YES, a week ago there was a funeral for a girl. She was 28 years old, she was very sick before she died. He showed me her grave, which was still covered with fresh flowers. Poor girl, it looked like she didn't know she was dead! She was walking among the living, a stranger trying to attract attention, but no one ever saw her!

Now I have a question for you: How many girls, especially a modern girl, a model, would go alone to the cemetery to talk to dead people, ghosts in the dark? Maybe one in 100, one in 500, maybe one in a million? I am sure no one will do this intentionally... I am sure the Priest in me went to the cemetery – not me. I still don't believe I did it.... Another one of those "inherited characteristics" to put on the list....

I remember that one of the girls I lived with always did the cleaning, wash the dishes, did the laundry – she was always working for everybody. One day she was up before everyone and wrote a note on a piece of paper:

"Please clean after yourself or I will kill you. Signed: Ghost."

You know what? Since that day, our apartment was squeaky clean....

Okay; back to that Japanese ghost girl.

My contract finished with that modeling agency and I moved to another area, working for another agency. And again there was a cemetery nearby! It was interesting that in Tokyo, the agencies put foreign people to live in places near cemeteries – because the rent was much cheaper. Tokyo has lots of old cemeteries right in the middle of town. This time, I was living in a wooden house on the second floor. During the weekend I visited a Japanese family in Yamanachi. Taky, his wife, Mammy, and I went to the South of Japan for two days. I returned from that trip with a big, green pray-mantis, which I kept in a cage. I was glad that the cemetery was nearby because it was the end of the summer and getting cooler and there were not too many insects left to feed the mantis. There was a time when I couldn't find any insect at all!

When I went to the cemetery to collect some insects for the mantis, I only saw a huge butterfly flying around some old tombs. I thought of what to do...? It is hard to kill such a beautiful creature to feed a mantis.... Yet, I thought the butterfly would die soon anyway since it was too cold for her and she was weak, but still so beautiful. I needed to spray her with some perfume to put her to sleep.... I couldn't do it.... It was very hard to start.... At that same moment, I remembered that my friend, Professor Taky, told me that a butterfly, in Japan, is the symbol of the dead people's spirit.... I brought it home. It was asleep, maybe it was dead already. I then took a needle, and when I stuck it in her heart, suddenly, the house started shaking! With a terrible sound!!!

I ran outside with the mantis in my hand. Many people came out as I did. I asked a neighbor, a Japanese woman: “Our house will fall down?”

She said, “Maybe not....” It had been a short earthquake tremor – 4.5 on the Richter scale.

Obviously for me it was a sign of punishment for the killing of this butterfly. Since that day and for a week afterwards I carried a bag with my passport, the ticket back to Canada, some money, and jewelry. It was the fourth earthquake in the last three months and I was worried that one day I would return to my apartment to find the house destroyed.

Soon, it was time to return to Canada. It was Friday, and I was flying home on Monday. I decided to go to buy some presents, souvenirs for my relatives and friends. I went to Yokohama, because they have everything there but much cheaper than in the middle of Tokyo. I remember I was in the sky train, sitting near an old Japanese man, who was carrying a very beautiful, hand-carved umbrella. Suddenly, I saw that he went out at the station and forgot his umbrella!

I was sure he loved this umbrella, and I ran out to try to find him, but he had disappeared in the crowd already! So, I dropped the umbrella at the “Lost and Found” place and continued my journey for a few more stations. When I arrived at my station I realized that I needed to pay some extra money for the trip. I went to an automatic exchange machine, but it was broken. Then, I went to make the change.... Anyway, when I was finally outside the station, instead of two things in my hands I had only one! I forgot my bag near that machine. I ran back.... no bag! I ran to the Lost and Found – but nothing!

My passport, tickets, money, everything valuable and important was in that bag! I called the police and asked them to see the tape of the security camera. We saw that a woman took the bag. The police told me that there was a mafia ring in this part of town, hunting for foreign documents and that they would probably re-sell my passport. I put an ad everywhere around that station, asking to return the passport, promising a reward - nothing. In the meantime, I was stuck in a hotel near the Canadian embassy, waiting for my new passport. Within a couple of days, they received all of my documents from Canada, but how could I prove that me was me? Some others could look exactly like me; conversely, I can look the same as someone else. They did it in a very smart way. I was asked the type of questions that only a Canadian living in that city would know. For example, they asked me how much is a bus ticket or general knowledge question such as, "What is the name for the dollar in Canada?"

"The Loonie," I replied, because on the Canadian dollar there is a picture of the magic loon, on its face.

I learned my lesson, though. Tourists should never carry their passports, only copies. It was very interesting when I had the interview. First, they showed me a plastic bag full of Canadian passports, stolen in that area. One passport was of a very nice looking woman – she killed her husband and two kids in some country and arrived in Japan, to buy a Canadian passport and to try to go to Canada. The second was that of a man, who was a drug dealer – he also arrived in Japan from somewhere else, trying to go to Canada.

The Priest

Anyway, three months later at the end of November, in Canada, I had a dream. That Japanese girl-ghost from the cemetery took me by the hand and brought me downstairs to some kind of basement. There was an empty, dark room. Inside, near the walls, there were bones of the dead people, each wrapped in some blankets. She brought me to the far left corner and opened one of the blankets. Inside, there was a scull and bones of the person who had presumably taken my passport since it was lying on its chest! She told me that the person who tried to use my passport was dead!

Perhaps the room where she brought me was under the cemetery. Maybe she wanted to show me how it looks under the ground in the world of the dead – her world . . . bones here, bones there.... Since then and for some 4 or 5 years she appeared in my dreams and delivered information about my life and my future. I have not seen her in the last few years.... But today when the fire alarm sounded, maybe it was her again... maybe I will see her in my dream today....

The Mexican Connections

There were interesting *coincidences* in connection with reincarnation that happened when I flew and arrived in Mexico, all of them occurred during the first 24 hours.

1. Numbers

On the way to the airport, all the cars around had license plates which had triple numbers! I gathered that the Universe or Mexican spirits tried to talk to me. It was some kind of coding with numbers 888, 444, 555, 111, 888, 555, 666, 444, 333, and they appeared repeatedly during the next 30 minutes. Our friend, Peter, my daughter and I didn't know what to think, what did it mean? Obviously, somebody was talking and trying to say something to us.

2. Hotel of Lord or King Pakal

When I arrived at the Cancun airport, it was late at night and there was only one hotel with rooms available. When I stepped inside, I felt as if I was a guest of the Lord or of King Pakal from Palenque Chiapas! This entire hotel was about him. His statues could be found inside and outside; there were beautiful bas-reliefs on the walls and even a fountain with his face carved at the base of it!

Hotel of Lord or King Pakal

Wow! I had heard that King Lord Pakal was reincarnated and lived now in Mexico. I wished to meet him one day! Maybe we will recognize each other. Maybe we were together in a past life.

3. Restaurant of reincarnation

Next stop, when we arrived in the morning at Acumal, I went to eat in the local restaurant. All of the statues and pictures on the walls were symbols of reincarnation and of spirits! I found big and small skeletons of humans, animals, and hundreds of calabashes, which the Mexicans keep as the containers of the Spirits.

The Priest

There were statues of strange animals on the beach such as I saw in a dream related to THE UPPER KINGDOM (Dream # 5) where there were goats and deer. They came out of the ocean in that dream...

Restaurant of the reincarnation
Calabashes – containers of the Spirits

Skeletons

4. Blessing by a Maya priest

While I was there, I saw a marriage ceremony starting on this beautiful, white, sandy beach. The Maya priest or maybe a shaman was conducting this ceremony and the blessing of the newly wedded couple. When he finished and passed near me, we felt some instant connection between us, which stopped him. What happened is impossible to explain. Although he couldn't speak English or Spanish – only Maya – he invited me to the beach and performed a full ceremony with a blessing connecting me with the God Kukulcan and other Maya Spirits. It was powerful and it touched me deeply.

Blessing by the Maya priest and shaman

5. Coba pyramid

The next day, early in the morning, I went to the Coba pyramid. I loved this ancient city. It was a pleasure to walk on the roads inside the forest with the amazing light going between the white-skin trees. I just enjoyed running up to the pyramid! I ran fast, without stopping and I even ran much faster coming down all these stairs! I did it a few times. I was very excited for some reason. It is impossible to explain how I felt. The tourists around were staring at me and took many photos of my running up and down the stairs..., because in order to come down from the pyramid they all crawled on their hands and knees like babies – that's how steep it was. It was not funny to see adult people in this embarrassing position. Yet, I was laughing, but I began showing them how easy it was to go down the stairs.

6. Rock from the past

The same day, I found a rock, which I believe was my favorite rock to play with as a Priest.

I was walking and I stopped suddenly. I felt it! I felt something very special in this place! I sat down and stretched my hand in front of me; it landed on this rock. Next: I took another, smaller rock and started to play – tapping the two rocks against each other. It all went automatically without thinking. My hands knew what to do. This white limestone rock produced the amazing sounds of crystal bells! I couldn't stop playing....

It is astonishing that this rock was waiting for me; no one had taken it or moved it in 2000 years! It was in a place, which is protected from any of nature's changes. I guess I started to feel my own energy in this rock, which I was playing daily, a long time ago for many years before meditation, to relax myself and to go into a trance.

We are calling this "energy", but according to scientist Peter Gariaev[20] it was my DNA phantom, which made an imprint on this rock many years ago. The same happened when I started walking for the first time in Chichen Itza and suddenly recognized everything around me, without even seeing the pyramids themselves. It was my phantom DNA which had stayed there since my past life and I started to be connected! By the way, I had a different DNA when I was a Priest. However, I guess, the phantom DNA soaked into the Spirit, making a print on my Spirit, which was reborn in my body. I continued playing on this rock now, every day. As I type this book, my feet are lying on my past, on this rock – on Mexican soil – I feel wonderful!

This rock is 38 by 25cm and the taxi driver at the airport asked me, "Why is your suitcase so heavy? You've got rocks in there or what?"
I replied, smiling from ear to ear, "YES, a very cool rock!" He didn't believe it, of course.

Tell me, how many people would you convince to take a rock to another country, which fills half of your suitcase and carry it thousands of miles away?

I guess it is impossible to find even another person like me. That's what I meant when I said there is NOTHING we could do about those characteristics we "inherited" from our relatives, like big ears, for example.... In my case, I *inherited* the Priest's love of the sounds from the rocks.

---

[20] You can read interpretation about this at the end of the book, "The Re-birth of an Atlantean Queen" by Julia SvadiHatra, in scientific section.

This rock produces sounds, which I made and heard in my past life, thousands of years ago as a Priest.... My Spirit remembers it and when I play again, it opens the door to my past life and the magic energy of the pyramid for me.

P.S.:
Many people love to travel to the same places. One of the reasons is that their DNA phantom leaves an imprint there and it is always a pleasure to restore your own energy with a fresh one, which is waiting for you to return. It works especially well with nature. It feels like that all of the trees, plants are saying “Hi” to you when you return and meet them again.

I don’t like delving in the ghost subject. In those places where people see ghosts, powerful DNA phantom exists from the time when someone produced strong emotions in the past. It occurs often in prisons, hospitals, cemeteries; places where people were sick and died, or in the houses they built and in locations where they invested lots of energy. At the moment people die, their body produces the strongest DNA phantom, I guess.

7. Statue

The first day I was in Chichen Itza, I woke up at 6 a.m. to be near the entrance at 7:45 a.m. I needed to take some photos for this book.

At 8:15 a.m., I was trying to take a good photo of the snake below the pyramid.

I was so excited that I did not pay attention and I stepped 20cm. inside the rope. The security guard ran to me instantly and brought me to the office. I was “punished”: I was not allowed to go inside the Chichen

Itza complex for the whole day. It would be a devastating feeling for someone who came from across the world and was supposed to stay away for one day. I was lucky that this time I was here for five days.

Everywhere there was a rope around the displays and it was impossible to take good photos. You could see the statue of Chak Mol, for example, only from far away...NO WAY to take a photo! But I needed his photo for the book for the next chapter!

The next day I woke up again at 5:30a.m. I went to the balcony to see the sunrise and guess what I saw. I could not believe my own eyes! In front of my room, on the grass, was the statue of Chak Mol! He was lying down, looking directly at me! I was so happy that I stayed in the Chichen Itza hotel, in Piste, in that room! What a lucky coincidence!

Chak Mol and Julia in the hotel garden

The Priest

This statue was a copy of the original, which was found a few years ago in the forest near Chichen Itza and the only one of which it was possible to take a photo! So I did!

8. Feelings

When I arrived in Chichen Itza, the second time, after my past life hypnosis readings, I was half Priest, half myself. This was what the Priest's Spirit inside me felt like in Chichen Itza. It was a deep, sad feeling I experienced from time to time. When I arrived, I was under a strong "Priest influence".... When I was near a pyramid, I felt as if it was my own home, *me casa...* my office....

I wanted . . . I needed to go inside. I wanted to touch this wall; I wanted to run up these steps.... I wanted to be near the Chak Mol's statue and I wished to burn incense on the red Jaguar's back at least once such as I did hundreds of times during my life as a Priest.... I wanted to touch that altar where my son laid down for the last time....

Sometimes, I had tears in my eyes.... The feelings near the pyramid were impossibly strong. As soon as I was near the pyramid, I had visions from my past life – real and bright....

At some point, I looked at tourists around through the Priest's eyes and I was glad that "ordinary people" did not walk in the sacred temple. Yes, the pyramid had been closed to the tourists for almost a year then. Yet, I felt that it was unfair: I was a Priest before and I lived and worked in this pyramid and now, I was reborn as a tourist and I just could not visit my own home. So, I went to Merida to obtain a special permit to take photos for the book. However and sadly, it takes a long time to obtain a permit, and it did not arrive until the day I left.

By the way, the body would die and the liberated soul (spirit) would set off the old ancestor, to get its new assignment at the right moment. Thus, together with a soul, a newborn baby inherits the social status, physical appearance and ancestral name of his (her) predecessor. ("Ancient America: flight in time and prostransive. Mezoamerika" Excerpts from the book by GG Ershovoy. Un-copyrighted@Sam, 2003-2006.)

I wish to visit the pyramid at least once!

Yet one thing which I enjoyed while I was a Priest and which warmed up my soul; there, I could play! I had a little, soft tennis ball in my pocket with a message, "The Priest Jaguar returns home," and I loved to spend time in the ball court . . . . I customized this ball to make it heavier than the normal ones.
I can't tell you more.

9. Equinox day

It was a very happy day for me! I was near the pyramid at 8:00 a.m. as usual. By the way, people who worked there asked me, "Why are you near the entrance every day at 7:45 a.m.? You are a tourist, but you're acting like you're coming here to work." It was my "office" before; my work was here and it looked like I used to wake up early to be at work on time....

Chichen Itza Pyramid, Julia, Equinox Day

During the Equinox Day, thousands of people arrived from all over the world – highly spiritual people.

I was near the pyramid and this feeling of responsibility and this sense of duty just did not leave me alone.... This is what I have in my mind – the Priest talked to me, "I need to be inside the temple... I need to have everything ready! Where are the gifts to the GOD? Where are the fruits, the Jewelry? How come no one will be there to meet and endorse the talk of the Spirit with the GOD when he will arrive? This is unruly.... It is impossible that there will be no prayers!"

I was staying near the stairs with presents in my bag, beautiful fruits, Lindor Easter Chocolates set in gold bunny and gold little animals and chicken eggs.

I felt really confused.... Suddenly, a little Maya girl, who just started to learn to walk, took her first steps toward me! I sat down and lifted this little doll to my knees. Her parents started to take pictures. I opened my perfume bottle; it was natural lilac oil, with a tender fragrance, and put one drop on the forehead of this little angel and one drop on each of her small, cute hands and blessed her. Next, some parents brought me a baby. After that, one parent brought to me another one...Wow! I was the happiest person in the whole of Chichen Itza! Finally, I was in the right place!

I just stayed near the stairs of my pyramid and blessed little children on this Holy Equinox Day – the same way I did two thousand years ago, exactly on the same day and at the same place. I was in great harmony with time and space. I was wearing a white and gold outfit for the hours of Celebration that day.

Later, I was walking near the pyramid when I started feeling some unusual energy at one particular place. There were beautiful tree blossoms, all of the flowers on those trees were like white lilacs, with the same fragrance I just used. I sat under those trees and waited. It was a hot day. Around me, there was something special with people, all of them wearing white clothes and sitting in total silence or talking very quietly.... It was a big contrast with the loud crowds around. At some point, they all stood up, all at once and started walking toward the pyramid to see the Equinox. I felt as if these people were a flock of white birds. I also started walking. Their spiritual teacher walked near me. His name was Julio Luis Rodriguez. He was a wise man, carrying a full face, wooden mask in his hands! Exactly the way I had dreamed, all my life! He told me that he felt a strong powerful energy emanating from me. Next, he put the mask on his face and saw me as a Maya princess... maybe it was my other life here in Mexico?

Mexican spiritual teacher, Julio Luis Rodriguez

Throughout the day, many people talked to me and told me that they felt a powerful energy around me. Yes, all of them felt the Priest Spirit, I guess – difficult to hide him. I saw many spiritual people visit the site on that day, people who could feel these kinds of things. I am sure they also have some special energy; otherwise, they would not have felt the strong Spirit in me, right?

Julia with Mexican artists, March 2008

Thousands of people arrived from all over the world for the Equinox day. I was amazed how well the Mexican government organized this event. Police, ambulances, soldiers, volunteers and scouts stood-by everywhere, ready to lend a hand with help and support. As you know during this day, I was in "the Priest's skin"; this event was my responsibility just a few thousand years ago. Mr. Jorge Esma Bazan, Director of Patronato Culture, State of Yucatan, Mexico and his team arrived and talked to the people from the stage. I went directly to them and told them that I was deeply grateful for their fantastic effort to keep the architectural complex of Chichen Itza in such an excellent shape, and I thanked them for the outstanding organization of such an important event as the Equinox day. They had no idea that this "Thank you" was not from an ordinary tourist but from one of the previous "rulers" of Chichen Itza, an ancient Priest.

Dream # 14
The grain of divinity, January 4, 1992

We knew the day, the hour and the place, where it would happen. And we were going there. Everything was prepared for this event. We calculated what day it should be. Pyramid.... When we came to the place, there were already thousands and thousands of people there. They all were looking. We arrived just at the very beginning. But not one of them knew what was going on.

At this moment, something came down from the sky. The Divinity. People were excited, scared of the strangeness of what was going on. The Divinity was somehow coming through the layers (of the atmosphere), became visible, but immediately, it fell apart into numerous pieces. But we knew what to do. We needed just one particle among them all. It was like a grain, like a sprout. The most important thing was in it. I knew, that we should take it and put it inside of what we already had, already prepared. Then our model would be complete and the pyramid would start working, would "wake up".

We were already assigned our responsibilities. First, you did something, and then I did it. I was transforming something into something else, which was becoming light and shining. And I also could name this grain. We knew exactly what to do, and we were doing it at the same time and in the same order as it was done far away in space. The specific outcome was the same. The same action at the same moment – simultaneously – we had to do it here, and them, there.

People around us were panicking; they did not understand what was happening. We were doing everything clearly, with a cold, calculating mind – we took the thing that approached us and did what we had to do. At this hour, this minute, this moment everything would change here, would be transformed. A fresh, new cycle would start. It would be the best possible outcome for all people. Suddenly, a wonderful, beautiful energy erupted in a burst of stars, like a huge energy fountain, came through the whole pyramid and went up to the sky, sending out Holy, glowing rays to all these people....They all saw it.

10. Spirit Support

I experienced the most amazing coincidence when I started writing this book. It felt as if someone was guiding me, watching over me. Suddenly, out of nowhere, I started receiving help with information, which arrived in the strangest form, from some of the most respectable sources. People around me began to be extremely cooperative and supportive.

Two days ago, I opened my entrance door at 6:30 p.m. and found, near the door, a DELL laptop! *Someone forgot a laptop near my door! Very strange!* I put a note to the person who forgot it there: "Why is your laptop here? Call me at this phone number. Please, come and take it back."

The next day my computer crashed, the hard drive was burned. I ran and bought a new laptop, but the technician told me that he needed a few days to transfer everything onto the new computer! This happened at the same time when my daughter was finishing school – we needed to fly to Europe soon, this book was almost done but I needed to work on it and complete it to give my editor, Roxane, for her to edit it, during the summer!

The Priest

I got a call from the next door neighbor, Tracy; he was the one who dropped the computer near the door! I asked him why? We don't know each other well enough, we only say, "Hi and Bye."

He replied, "I don't know. Something in my mind pushed me to go to my locker room, find this computer and bring it to your door. I thought that since I stopped using it, maybe someone like your daughter would like to use it!"

(Well, my daughter has a good computer.)

Yet, since I just experienced unexpected delays, I guess I could use it for a few days to complete the book! What a great help! Today, I got my new laptop ready to work. Tracy's laptop went to my daughter, she is very happy. It is a nice laptop, working very well! But most importantly she can use it anywhere in her room. She can download songs and learn to play them on the sofa – while not using her desk near her big computer screen. Thank you Tracy!

As for me, I am thinking about this Spirit, who is really watching me and is trying to help even in situations like these. Spirits know ahead of time what will happen and they support us as much as possible. My Spirit helped me in such a way that I could complete this book as soon as possible so to make it available to people!

Here is Tracy's version of the "Laptop Mystery":

About a week ago I decided to go to my locker room for no special reason. There, I saw my laptop and decided to give it to my neighbor's little girl. I felt that she might want it – or need it. So I dropped the laptop near the door of my neighbors, Julia and her daughter. Julia found the laptop a few hours later. She didn't know who brought the laptop at first but when she realized that it was me, she wrote me a thank you note saying that she didn't need it because her daughter had a good computer now. However, the next morning Julia's own computer suddenly crashed! She ran to buy a new laptop, but the technician wanted to take a few days to put all the data from the old computer onto the new one and took both computers away from her.

Well, suddenly my laptop became the most important item for Julia, because (and I found this out later) she needed to finish this book before flying to Europe with her daughter for the summer! I am still not sure why I went to the locker room that day – there was no reason for me to do so. I was watching TV after work and I just stood up, went to the storage room, took out the laptop and brought it in front of Julia's door. I acted like a robot or zombie.... It may sound funny, but this is exactly how it happened. I thought about this strange situation for a while – I guess Julia has a guardian angel which takes good care of her, helping her.

By the way, around a month ago, on our floor, there was an odd fire alarm in the hallway and it would not stop. I ran to the manager. We were ready to call for the fire truck after we checked everything and did not find any reason for the insistent ringing. Julia also went outside with her daughter and their little ferret. When I told her that we could not find any reason for the alarm, she told me that she was writing a chapter in her book right then, which was dealing with a ghost girl! She thought the ghost might have activated the alarm, trying to make her presence felt.... It sounds really weird, but after my unexplainable trip to the locker room, I started to think that everything is possible when it comes to Julia. Something special, magic exists around her. Each time I see them, my good mood returns, even when I come home and I am very tired after a long day's work.

Tracy Graig, Vancouver, Canada

I should mention here that I had previous experiences with Spirit support in my life. Once I bought a manuscript from China about the ancient Chi Gong form of exercises. In that book I found some "well-guarded" secrets, giving the reader guidance in order to put you into a trance so that your body would start moving by itself, which, in turn, could also produce some powerful healing. It is all about how the body wishes to move, and not how our brain decides to move our body. I was planning to publish this book and decided to try the exercises myself first. It did not go the way it should have done – my body movements were still guided by my will, I just couldn't grasp the process. Later, I visited my business partner, C.P., in San Diego. He has a beautiful private Buddhist temple with a golden Buddha and ancient statues on his property. It was a rare opportunity for me to meditate in the temple alone. I asked him if I could spend the night there. He told me that there were some spirits who lived in the temple and that no one had expressed the wish to be there alone before that day – people were generally afraid, he said. I asked, "What kind of Spirit?"

C.P. told me that monks had meditated all their lives in the temple and their brain created a strong electromagnetic energy flow within it. It had built-up over the years in the "salige" – two little white bones in their brain, which normal, ordinary people never have! The monks collect the "salige" after the cremation. In the Buddhist temples, it is a tradition to put the *saliges* of the deceased monks in a special type of containers. When many monks prayed near the little waterfall in one of the temples, C.P. saw a special, white sand, some kind of substance on the rocks around this waterfall. They explained to him that it was because of the constant meditations performed by the monks in that place over the years.

So, in his private temple, C.P. had the "salige" from a high ranking monk who lived a very long life – as I remember, around 123 years. Apparently, this Spirit came from time to time for a visit, because his "salige" was located in that private temple. He showed it to me, in a little silver container. The shape of the container was very familiar to me. I had seen the same in Tibet in my childhood. While C.P. was talking to me, suddenly his eyes began to focus on something in front of him, his head started to move very fast, and I saw something really strange and unusual in the air between us. It looked like a cloud of bees or black dots, of about a meter in length. This cloud was moving back and forth at great speed for some time, and suddenly it disappeared. He told me that the monk's Spirit had been near us.

I woke up in the early morning hours before sunrise in that temple – no one had bothered me during the night – and I started meditating. After my meditation, I remembered the Chi Gong exercises and decided to try it this time. Nothing good came from this idea again, and I almost gave up. Then, I decided to call on someone "in the know" – I called on the Spirit of the monk and asked him to help. Since this ancient exercise was originally from Tibet, I figured that he would have known how to perform these exercises during his lifetime. Suddenly, a voice came to my mind: "Hold on. Let's try it again," he said. It was an astonishing experience! I returned to reality maybe 40 minutes later. During this time I only felt that my spine turned into a powerful energy flow, like a thick rope, which was going through me and I felt the dynamic, electric movement of it. What I felt was incredible – both during and after the exercise. Since then, from time to time, I call on this Spirit, when I need him.

Every time, I can feel his presence strongly, no matter in which part of the world I happen to be.

****

Once I was the object of a sacrifice.

On that particular evening, I was walking through a district amid crowds of people. I felt happy and wonderful about myself. The spring had made its appearance and it was the first warm days. I was wearing a new outfit: white, and quite in fashion at the time. I was a very naive young girl, who was just beginning to make her entrance in the world of adults. Suddenly, out of nowhere, a man appeared near me and he began following me. I tried everything possible and impossible, but I just couldn't get rid of him. At one point, he stopped right in front of me, and I didn't have any way to escape. Then, I saw a woman near her car on the side of the road, waving to me. I don't remember exactly what she screamed to me, but it was something like, "Step here, on the other side and you will be rid of him; he will go on his way."

I took a few steps towards her and that car... and as soon as I was near, a hand from inside the car pulled me with powerful force into it! The door was slammed and the car left at great speed. I felt a knife touching my ribs and then one of these two men put some cuffs on my ankles. Meanwhile, the car kept going and I could see that we were going out of town. At one point, the car stopped and the man who had put the cuffs on my ankles got out and went into another car and left. I was left alone with the driver. I asked him, "Where are we going?" – It was dark outside and I could only see the forest.... He did not answer. He continued driving silently.

Finally we arrived. We had been driving along a highway – not much traffic. He pulled into a small crossroad and drove perhaps 50 meters onto that road. We stopped and waited. Suddenly, he started talking. He told me that today was a very special day for him, because he was part of what I call now an "association". (I don't want to say where it happened, what country and what year, because this story is too terrible to tell.) Once a year there was a big celebration with a sacrifice! For this sacrifice it was necessary to have a young, beautiful woman.... And I was the one who had been chosen for the sacrifice on that day!

It was a special day for him personally, because by participating in my kidnapping, he would be lifted to the next rung on the step ladder in that "association". He told me that I should not be scared; instead I should be very proud to be part of it! Because I was to see elite people from high society, and some I would recognize: politicians, business people, celebrities and even top level religious figures from two different organizations ... and that my body was to be used for such an important ritual....

Can you believe it? At first, I was sure that he was a schizophrenic or a paranoiac..., because he was obviously under stress and I saw that his hands were shaking.... But after he started showing me a huge size white candle, I knew he was serious. He repeated again that today he would be "endorsed" and would attain a new status in that "association" and this day was very important for him.

Well, it sounded as if his job also consisted in preparing the victim emotionally. I asked him if they use something to sedate their victim to keep it calm and cooperative. He was amazed that I, instead of screaming and crying, was talking to him about the details of this procedure. He asked me why I was like this.

As for me, I thought it was better to spend time before my death thinking about my life, the results I had achieved, and maybe say goodbye to my relatives than losing my mind and screaming. People who scream in such stressful situations always create chaos and the situation can get easily out of control. These people can be killed first and fast, simply in order to shut them up.

I continued talking to him. I asked him if he had any family. He told me that he had only a three-year-old daughter – no mother. He then told me how much he loved her and showed me her photo. I smiled at that point, which had a strange effect on him – his facial expression changed and he went out of the car to smoke a cigarette. He went and opened the trunk of the car looking for something. I was sitting in the car alone. When I saw him opening the trunk, and before he closed it, I threw the big candle out of the window as far as I could into the brush nearby. To date I have no explanation as to why I did this. It was like someone took my hand and moved it, as if I was a puppet. Very mechanical move....

He returned inside and checked his watch. He told me that soon a car will arrive to pick me up for the preparation – "it will be time for us to go," he said. At that point, he started looking for the candle and of course he couldn't find it! He looked everywhere – he turned the whole car upside down.... Nothing....
He then turn to me and said, "Why you didn't ask me about my wife, my daughter's mother?

"My wife was killed one year ago by the car on the road exactly at the same street where we caught you today, around the same place! And when you started smiling while I was talking about my daughter I saw that you have exactly the same smile as my wife had! And now the candle disappeared... this is a really bad sign....

"Emotionally I tried to be prepared for my participation in the sacrifices for a long time. I was told that I just need to go through it.... But after all that happened tonight and no candle... I am not sure that I am doing the right thing!"

He was under so much stress that his hands were shaking and he even started smoking again inside the car....

Suddenly he pointed to the road ahead. I saw a long, black limo coming on the main road towards us. He had already shut down all the lights in and outside our car before then, and now he whispered, "I will not give you up to them to be killed. I made my decision. They should not see us."

The limo waited for about 20 or 30 minutes and then left. When we were sure that the limo was totally out of sight, he asked me, "Where do you live?" I didn't want to tell him, instead I asked him to drop me off downtown.

I never saw him again. But I know that that strange, unexpected movement of my hand, which threw the candle into the darkness, saved my life. Who was it? My guardian angel? Or maybe the Priest in me knew exactly what to do and that this candle was the key to my freedom? I still don't know. This Spirit saved my life. By the way, when I told this story in detail to my cousin, the next day, a stripe of white hair appeared on this boy's head by the end of my account. I have never seen such a thing in my life – someone's body reacted so strongly and visibly to shock!

****

What people around are saying about the Priest's connections and my habits in this present life.

I don't know Julia very well. I have seen her 2 or 3 times at the Chinese New Year. We started talking with her about her cute ferret that she always has with her. I give her advice regarding homeopathy for the ferret.

We decided to meet again for a short meeting. I wished to give her very nice spiritual book about my teacher, Tulshi Sen. Our first meeting, on Sunday at 9 a.m. was at English Bay. We talked and walked near the road. Julia mentioned that numbers play an important part in her life. They kind of speak to her. When she had a question or thought about something and tried to make a decision, her numbers started showing up. If it was a lucky number, she knew that her decision was correct. Or if her bad numbers started showing up it meant that she should avoid something. I listened to this and told her that I too have a lucky number, it is #13.

While we were walking near the road, at the crossing of Beach Avenue and Davie, we were close to the main entrance to the beach. The street was empty, it was a Sunday morning and suddenly one car arrived and stopped near the crossing and the car license plate number was 013.

Next, the following car came and its license plate was also # 013! It stopped after the first one. A third car arrived with the same number 013 on the license plate! All three cars stayed one after the other: 013, 013, 013!

She pointed and said to me, "See! Again, as usual! All my business partners know this... it happened when I was in the cars in South Korea, or Los Angeles, or

Moscow or Japan or London or Hawaii or anywhere in the world." I was in shock and didn't know what to think.

The Universe really speaks to her and proved to me that YES some high power is talking with her! It was an astonishing feeling and kind of scary. How it can be possible that someone sent at the same moment 3 cars with the same number right at the same time that we were discussing it...? These cars arrived from the road, which goes through the park and there was not much traffic as it was not a busy time of the day. For three cars to arrive simultaneously with the same number, it is impossible to understand. It is impossible to understand with our logical mind, it has to be felt with your heart.

I know that the Universe keeps talking to us using every media possible, but it can use language that we are able to understand. In Julia's case numbers are one of the media, she really tuned into. There is a very special aura around her; it is really hard not to notice the higher energy levels in her presence. I met her again, after about a year had passed, and decided to mention this incident in the book she is writing.

Istvan Orodan, Vancouver, Canada

****

This is just an example of one day in Julia's life... In October 2007; I was driving Julia, to the airport as she was catching a flight to Spain. When we arrive I looked down at the odometer, which I had reset at some point earlier in the week. However, as I was there and the exact distance that I had traveled since resetting it was at 87.7km, which is usually a negative number, that Julia has always mentioned and always appears just before some kind of trouble. Obviously, it was a warning sign for her. She asked me to wait and give her a few minutes to think. She continued walking into the airport building. She returned almost instantly and told me: "I will not fly, I want to go back home now". I was literally shocked by her immediate decision!

On the way back in to town, she told us that at the moment when she started thinking about the possibility of not to flying that day, she started feeling easy and light, as if she was in heaven. It's like she ran away from hell or from some terrible disaster – like a weight was lifted off her shoulders.

The next day we learned that horrible, severe flooding had started during her scheduled flight in this area and by the time she would have arrived in Spain, 14 hours later, all the roads were washed away, they were closed by flooding, and the bridge over the river collapsed in Alicante, where she should have landed. This caused huge damage and people were dead and missing.

The Universe or some higher power protected her, like a guardian angel speaking to her through numbers and prevented her from taking this deadly trip. Those numbers on that day could have saved her life or obviously from lots of stress. I feel now that it will be safe for anyone to be near her, because she has some high power protecting her and those around her.

Shawn, Canada

****

I didn't know Julia before I started editing her manuscript. For some reason, she insisted that I edit her book. I was swamped – I had work coming out of my ears (as the saying goes) and I had no intention to take on another project. However, when I read the translation of some of her dreams, I was intrigued. What is this all about? Where does she want to go with this? I had no answer to these questions until I decided that I could plough through this bunch of dreams and visions over the summer months, while Julia was away. And then it began – my other work, either fell by the wayside or no other clients came knocking. I found myself working exclusively for Julia! To date, I have only one book on the table – hers. It is as if everyone is waiting in the wings for me to finish this project before approaching me again. A good example of this, is the fact that one of my new clients wrote an email to me a couple of weeks ago, saying that she had unexpected visitors for three days, and because of this, she would be delayed for another two weeks or so before she could send me her manuscript. That came as a shock – I can't survive on only one client – even one of Julia's caliber. When I told Julia about this, she said, "Don't worry, we will be soon in Mercury Retrograde, which is a great time for finishing big projects and not starting new ones – but previous clients will show up!" That's all fine and dandy, I thought, but who's going to feed me in the meantime? I have absolutely no idea what "Mercury Retrograde" is or means – I live a simple, down to earth kind of life. Nevertheless, I trusted her instincts and let it go at that. The amazing thing about this is that it does not concern me in the least – I knew that the minute I'd "put this baby to bed"; the phone would start ringing again.

And yes, it happened exactly as Julia had predicted it. I got two people wanting my help with some editing as soon as I closed her book. On top of this, while we were talking about future publishing plans, when I was walking with her down the street, a car with her lucky number – 085 – crossed the intersection in front of us.

For all of you who read this book, let me tell you something; Julia is a true to life visionary and a superb scientist to boot. Every one is "one of a kind" as she says, but she is the "real" thing!

The Priest

Roxane Christ, Vancouver

****

My sister, Julia, visited me and my family, in Germany. She lives in Canada and I live in Europe. After many years of living apart, we decided to meet and go to town to celebrate this event in some fancy restaurant.

To my surprise on such a special and happy occasion, instead of wearing one of her many luxurious and glamorous outfits, she chose to wear her jaguar jacket and she even attached a tail to it for fun! I noticed she even had a jaguar mask in her hands!

I felt really uncomfortable by this and I started to tell my husband that I was afraid that people around us would think that we hired her as the entertainment person. I love her, but that evening I felt really ashamed for her. She, instead, was extremely happy with this jacket – she was always wearing it and I guess could even sleep in it. It was a quality garment, the kind of silk like jacket from "Victoria's secret catalogue". Still, I couldn't take it. I didn't understand why it made her feel so excited and happy or why she was so attached to it. Anyway, I asked her remove the tail at least, and not to use the mask. After all that, the celebration on the day was a very happy time for us!

Elena Neimark, Germany

****

Julia loves leopard and jaguar print clothing. Every Halloween she wears this outfit. It makes her extremely happy! It seems to make her happy to have the opportunity to wear a jaguar costume once a year. She walks around with a jaguar mask, long tail, and jaguar print gloves – the entire costume. She is always a Jaguar. Every Halloween she gets lots of candies for wearing a costume! People love her outfit. It is always fun lots or joy for kids to be near her. I guess she was even offered a free home at the "big cat" reserve in California.

Mitchell Van Hartevelt, Canada

****

I am a professional journalist and writer in the genre of science fiction. I have known Julia for many years. As our relationship formed and grew, Julia confided in me and she began to tell me her own dreams. I listened to these dreams and was very puzzled by them. They were always very detailed, and it was impossible to imagine them coming from events of a regular, normal life. These dreams were always new and unusual, and there was the impression that they have a deep reason, with a certain inexhaustible source of information.

As a journalist, I use the technique of quick record, with elements of shorthand. I had a professional interest, as I thought that I would be able to use this in my future books. This was of great interest to me and I thought my readers would find them to be very interesting as well. The intensive hand-writing, about an hour a day, was a rather grueling procedure. Her dreams were vast and full of details. It didn't take long for me to realize the difficulty of this process as it went from day to day, (every morning, soon after she woke up, and also sometimes after her usual middle-day nap) into months and over many years. As a result I presently have several handwritten folios filled with notes and drawings. In these dreams there were a lot of repeated events. They included such things as pyramids, crystals, unusually large people, and ceremonies with large crowds of people participating, strange energy rituals, stairways, person with unusual tattoos, hands with mandala-like tattoos, snow-white beaches, turquoise water, beautiful palaces with spherical roofs, and even strange energy essences. The general intonation of these dreams, and the events described in them, brought me to believe that all this is about cultures of ancient Greece, ancient Egypt or something even much more ancient like Atlantis or Sumerian.

Julia sometimes when awake, she repeated words in strange languages. No one knows the meanings or has any idea as to the kind of language it is. The word "equinox" is often repeated in her mind after her dreams. There was the sense that some parts of her lives were in another, as if in a parallel life. These images were so bright, alive and realistic.

Recently she has visited Mexico. At the architectural complex in Chichen Itza, Julia suddenly began to recognize the surrounding structures. They all seemed very familiar to her-pyramids, stairways, details and the general atmosphere of this place. On her return to Canada, Julia went to a specialist on regressive hypnosis. It was here that all the pieces fell into place, like small parts of a puzzle. During these sessions she lapsed back to memories of her previous life, and she realized that she was a High Maya priest, who performed ceremonies and rituals on top of the pyramid. These procedures were witnessed by crowds of people. The main ritual was conducted at the moment of the Equinox!

Today, speculating recorded dreams, information received during hypnosis, as well as the events of her present life, I understand that they are all interconnected. Many belongings of the past life are unconsciously repeated in her present. In her dress, in appearance she unconsciously had the habits to past life: being High Priest, she carried the long cape from the skin and mask of the jaguar. Presently she loves color and patterns, drawing of the skin of the jaguar, she adores masks, as well as embellishment "accustomed" on past life: jewelry from sinks, big stones, chosen bone, seeds, feathers, heavy bracelets on her hands and legs, heavy rings on her fingers, etc. As if she is in the costume of the previous life.

In her past life, as a High Priest and Astrologer, she was also in charge of agricultural science. In her present life she became a biologist, specializing in agricultural science.

She is also presently very interested in astrology, which has become more than a hobby. In the former Soviet Union, during "Perestroika" she put a lot of her efforts and energy into the legalization of astrology, which was previously forbidden in USSR. One of the first astrology books in USSR was released with her help. Interestingly, in the list of authors, Julia's name is not used, but instead, as we now know, the name used was that of the High Maya Priest, Magician. At the time she did not have any idea what Magician meant, from where this word came from, she just created this word because she said she felt harmony with it.
Mayan people were a great mathematicians and astrologers, they extensively used calculations. In Julia's present life, numbers play an enormous and mystical role for her, just as if they "talk" to her in some way. There are certain numerals, some of which serve as warning signs about problems lying ahead, or provide negative answers to given questions. The other numerals correspond to the favorable answers or indicate successful outcomes. These numerals can be anywhere, commencing from license plates of passing vehicles, commercial banners, phone numbers or addresses. The most amazing part is that when questioned, numbers suddenly show up not just one or two, but repeatedly in much larger amounts than in normal, possible situations.

The Priest

For example, it can be 5-8 cars with the same number around at the same time.

Tim, Russia (Julia's ex-husband)

PS: When I heard her repeating the words, when she woke up, I tried to type them, but they were incomprehensible to both of us.[21]

****

WHO AM I?

I asked myself "WHO AM I?" a few months ago. You just finished reading who emerged from this question during the hypnosis sessions and after using Dr. Alfons Ven's "miracle pills". First the Priest came out, and now see who else will come in the next chapters.... I am planning to check some more dreams with Di Cherry's help and see who else I was in my past lives.

I guess I could be a good Buddhist if I continued to follow this road of self development properly. Buddha always asked to look at your self and to study your self first.

I just returned from the beautiful Stanley Park, everything is blooming there! And again I was talking to the animals today. I caught myself talking to a raccoon – after I heard my voice: "So how are you today? What do you do? What do you eat?" It just came automatically – this contact, this instant connection – as soon as I saw the raccoon, I talked to him.

---

[21] You will find scientific Interpretation about this at the end of the book, "The Re-birth of an Atlantean Queen", by Julia SvadiHatra.

"Oh, hi, doc, what a cute baby you have! And you are such a gorgeous swan! I love those shiny diamond drops of water on your back!" Suddenly, a huge carp jumped out of the water, so high that I could see its full size with its yellow tummy and belly. "Bravo! Bravo! Bravo carp!" I clapped my hands. *Am I crazy?*

These animals saw me from far away and started running toward me – all of them – and they followed me; the squirrel and geese, the swan, the raccoon. I was running then, down one of my favorite trails in the park. This time I had my camera with me. When we stopped, I told the squirrel: "Just stay this way; I will do your profile. You will be a movie star!" She sat, didn't move and I took her photo. Then I came closer and closer, and she still sat and didn't move – she stayed in the same position for a long while – "Good squirrel!" I said.

But something was wrong! After a few minutes she was still sitting in the same position.... She was literally frozen. I ended up touching her with the camera lens, but she just continued to sit! What a strange squirrel!

By this time I was near the lake, named The Lost Lagoon, and I saw him – my cute raccoon, walking softly near the water. I continued playing the same game. I told him, "Now your turn. You stay in profile and I will take your portrait." The raccoon stopped, turned his profile towards me.... "And don't move.... Very nice!" I got many photos with my camera.... This camera is not a fast kind of camera; by the way, it's just a normal Canon camera – after each shot you need to wait a little bit... But the raccoon still didn't move! He stayed in the same position!

All of a sudden, I heard a man's voice behind me, saying, "Look, the raccoon is posing for this girl, can you believe it?"

"Look! He is frozen!" he added.

Yes. He was frozen! Like the squirrel before him, and I just didn't know what was going on. Almost five minutes had passed since I took his photo – according to the camera time – and he stayed like this.... Well..., this is kind of strange, very strange. "Bye, raccoon! See you next time," I said, walking away.
After that I called the swan – same story!!! I returned home and started taking pictures of my neighbor's cat, exactly the same thing occurred . . . AGAIN!
All of these animals were frozen on the spot after I took their pictures. All of these animals understood what I told them to do and just did it!

Raccoon posing

Squirrel posing

This wild cat only approached Julia and touched her hand

The Priest

When I started showing the photos to an old professional photographer, who always hung out around this lake, he just could not believe his own eyes! He told me that these are wild animals, "this is impossible...no one could train them to do this." We both didn't know what to think of it. I guess the Priest knew what this was all about. He had a close connection with nature, animals, plants, birds; he was part of all this!

Since I connected with the Priest, I feel that his qualities add to those I had already.[22]

It feels like somebody inside me turns on a computer and I know instantly what to do, where to go and what I can expect there. I am doing things now before thinking about them. And I don't make any mistakes – Not One.

It reminds me very much of those robots with sharp ears from the "Terminator" movie. My thoughts and

---

[22] *I was jogging in the forest when I saw on the trail ahead of me a large coyote. I stopped and waited for him to clear the way. Another man approached and also waited. Just last week, that coyote attacked a woman with a baby and killed some raccoons in this area. As soon as the coyote walked away from the trail we tried to go through as fast as possible. When I turned back I saw a girl behind me – she was going directly to the coyote and even called him! The coyote started walking toward her and they stood close, almost touching each other! After that she started walking in our direction... When I asked her if she was totally out of her mind, she smiled and told us that she found the coyote very beautiful, especially his eyes.... I was surprised how confident and calm she was. I was shivering. She told me that she had a good connection with animals because her great-grandfather was a Maya Priest.*
She said that I could send her a note about this incident for her book. Well... she has long blond hair and obviously, she is European... But anyway, here is my report about this odd case...
Henry M.

movements of the body are honed to a fine point, they are clear and focused. My ability to make a fast, instant and correct decision amazes normal people. I am starting to have much stronger intuition. My survival instinct is extremely high. I am very well organized and I have a cool mind in stressful or dangerous situations.

I know the source of it all now. I had the opportunity to exercise all of this in my past lives. Now and after establishing a connection with my past, all these extra skills and abilities are activated, start working inside me. It's like I have three brains in one now: mine, the Priest's and the one from the Atlantean woman. It's good that I started controlling my mind since I was very young to keep a clear head and away from the society stereotypes while saving space to add another two brains.

All of the people around me noticed these changes. But they don't know what it is.

In Mexico I saw a blanket with a picture of my pyramid. I ran into the shop and bought it – without thinking. An hour later I decided to move to another hotel on the Rivera Maya, located on the white beach near Tulum – a beautiful place! BUT the wind picked up and I needed my new blanket more than anything in the world that night.

The artist just called me while I was typing something about the cover for this book. I picked up the phone and told him his name – even before he said "Hello". I just knew it was him on the line. He was surprised – me too – this was our first talk, at least in this lifetime.

Yesterday evening, I was walking down the street when suddenly, out of nowhere, two teenagers jumped in front of me and started screaming, trying to impress a bunch of teenage girls nearby. I felt this movement before it happened. I lifted my hand to stop them and to show them that I was aware of their intention. I told them, smiling, "No way! You can't scare me, Never! It was good for nothing!" They were surprised, and decided that I was "cool".

Yes, I agree, this Priest is really cool! I continue to be surprised by his abilities every day.

Now, when I walk in the park everyday, my body moves like that of the Priest – adopting a kind of animal, soft, rounded walk. This is how energy flows through my body now. No straight legs, artificial, human walk anymore. I am part of nature now. I see the road far ahead and I know, ahead of time, who will come out of the bushes, who will cross the road: raccoon or people or . . . spirits....

Two days ago I walked near the golf course; suddenly I lifted my hand automatically without thinking, and caught the ball that was heading for my face! Balls fly over the fence through the bushes all the time but this time it was aimed at my head! The astonishing thing was that it was not I who moved my hand – I didn't have time to realize that a ball was going to hit me. It was a very unusual kind of movement, like a pray-mantis does. Yes, this Priest is pretty cool; otherwise I would have ended up with blue bruises on my cheek, or a black eye!

Today I started thinking about the parameters of the wisdom, which I mention throughout the book, and which comes to me at the appropriate moment.

It feels as if I do not belong to some particular society, nationality, country or race anymore. Instead, I feel an attachment to the whole Universe and humanity with the warmest feelings toward nature: plants, animals, birds, insects and even crystals, or rocks. It gives me an incredible sense of harmony and comfort to feel that I am a little part of the living space around me – mountains, ocean, and valleys. Usually people think before they speak. Right?

However now, I can instantly express my thoughts in words without aforethought. It means that I often speak with synchronic thinking – my thoughts and speech are synchronized – no prior thinking. I also write at the same speed as my thoughts come to mind, and I talk without spending time choosing the words. It seems that the frequency of the working brain and the speaking channels are in great harmony. I think this is what I experienced at the Buddhist temple, when the monks were playing the drums. They have the same perfect correlation, and coordination between their brains and hand movements.

Three years ago, while I was at the temple, I remember the top monk mentioning the rare possibility of Chi energy residing in our brain. Perhaps the vibrations of my body reach the same level as that of the vibrations of my Spirit. I experienced the same thing in my dreams – Spirit is in incredible harmony with all that I just mentioned. Now, in real life, I am beginning to experience the same astonishing moments such as I only experienced in my dreams before.

A few days ago, I started paying attention, analyzing and comparing myself with people around me, on TV, and on the street. I found that in my thoughts and actions, in my emotions or in those minute wishes, personal likes or dislikes never rule or affect the situation in which I may be at the time. The feelings or apprehensive worries just no longer exist. However, I still say what I feel, directly and instantly, about things I don't like.

I noticed that I enjoy life much more now, yet, in a different way than the way millions of people do. In most cases, their activities seem flat and empty to me, if they are not connected with nature. As for my lifestyle, people may think that my life is boring. I can compare this opinion with the life of an uneducated person – a person who never realized how empty and boring his life is without knowledge, or with the life of those poor kids in Africa, who are eating only one kind of food during their entire life. They never had the possibility to taste something else. They are living in little mud shacks in the desert – no fun, no trees, no water to swim or play, no knowledge, no sharing of information. Everything around them is only one grey, yellow, muddy landscape. They are lucky of just one thing: they will never know how bad their life actually is, because they will never have the possibility to compare their life with anything else.

For me, those moments of enlightenment and connection with the Universe are astonishingly beautiful, deep, valuable, multidimensional and priceless. I cannot compare these moments with any kind of entertainment or pleasure people enjoy here on Earth. It is free, open, and it can be reachable. Everyone, including these poor children, can attain this state of inner happiness.

Once, many years ago, during a "charity week" at Christmas time, I was visiting gifted people, kids, who were sick and poor people in Moscow. I shared some precious moments with them and donated my own money. I was a successful and wealthy entrepreneur at the time, and a pioneer in charity organization – no one was doing this sort of thing in Russia then. Newspapers even wrote articles about this new "invention". I remember meeting a talented boy who was paralyzed. He was spending his life in bed, at home. He had no friends, no fun. I brought him lots of spiritual books, and at the moment I was about to say goodbye, suddenly, I told him one sentence, "Your body is stuck, frozen here on Earth, but your Spirit is *Free* and you can travel in your dream far, far away." A few weeks later, his mother called me and asked me to visit him again. Amazingly, he had changed – he was transformed! His face glowed with happiness and excitement; he smiled and started describing to me his visits to different planets and stars! He easily described the atmospheric pressure, the minerals, some circles, and all kinds of physical characteristics that this planet displayed, in infinite details! I understood then, that in his unique situation, being excluded from all activities, which ordinary people have in their daily routine, he could afford to spend days, months of training, and focus his mind on only one goal: travel the Universe. He attained incredible results and most importantly, he now felt extremely happy and complete!

I asked myself "WHO AM I?" a few months ago. It may be a good idea for you to ask the same question of yourself. What you will discover may be very intriguing!

The Priest

Who am I?

Photo by Tim Orden www.timorden.com tim@timorden.com Phone: 808 620-8876

Julia has been to Mexico and now she blossomed spiritually since she returned!
Her enthusiasm soars like a beautiful bird! Some magic occurred between her and this pyramid! - You can feel the difference and hear it in her voice. You can see that even animals understand and follow her now! Her intelligence is beyond belief and she must be an old soul as she knows more than most people could comprehend. She strongly connected with the Energy from the Universe. But now she is full of Wisdom.

Carol, Edmonton

***

When I woke up today, I continued talking in some ancient language, repeating some words over and over again. A Deep Global voice was talking into my ears. My temperature rose and this was a sign of importance. I still felt the presence of people and spirits around me from my dream..., and I tried to write this down very fast.... My body was covered with goose bumps.... I started to remember....

Dream # 15.
A message from the Magnificent Maya people, June 24, 2008

I was up in the temple, standing near the entrance, and looked down. Everything was under the golden sunset light. I see the Temple of Warriors. Hundreds of warriors were standing on the bright red stairs. One by one, in total silence, all of them looking at me up here. Short skirts, belts, necklaces and spears reflected the sunset light.... I saw the sunlight going through their eyes. I saw their shiny black hair, toned legs and arms' muscles.... Columns made a long shadow....

I felt that my astrologers in the Caracol were also frozen in time.... I saw Maya people sitting on the ground around the pyramid with their children, wives and old parents.... These are all my people... I know each and everyone of them. I blessed them when they were born and when they were married. Many came to me for help when they were sick, or for support and advice. This is my Big Family.

I turned back and looked inside the temple. My old teacher, the Priest, is sitting with his tortoise in his hands. All my people were around me dressed in beautiful, colorful outfits with feathers, masks and shiny, luxurious jewelry. The Snake, the Eagle and Anubis were nearby as usual. They all looked at me very seriously – they were waiting in total silence. From the corner of my eye, I saw long, tall figures, watching all of us in the distance.

It felt as if TIME had stopped and they were all frozen in that moment.... All these people were cut and separated from us and our time....

Something in between ... in between times ... and it was burning. I saw a big fire. I looked closely. It was literally mountains of ancient books and manuscripts burning in this fire! I saw some manuscripts that were very deep at the bottom of the dark ocean, that were covered with sand, near parts of a wooden *baroque*-styled ship.

Then I receive the message...

****

Now I will try to tell the message. I am not sure that people will be able to understand what this message means, especially since it was given to me in ancient Maya. I will try some simple modern way and in English – although English is not my native language....

As a High Priest of Chichen Itza from ancient Mayan people to each human been living on Earth: -

I am re-incarnated after thousands of years, maybe to give you a message in the special time of ending of 13-baktun cycle.

Chichen Itza is not just another tourist attraction.

This city is where my people, my family, my friends lived beautiful, bright, happy lives. People were creative and deeply spiritual. The ancient Mayan people who built

Chichen Itza had highly developed culture, science, architecture, astronomy, most advanced astrology and were in constant connection with God and with the parallel world in space.

We lived in great Harmony with the Energy of our Planet, Space, Sound, Plants, Animals, Rocks and Ocean. Some of us had the ability to travel in time and we accumulated the most valuable information as a precious gift to the human race. What people know now about ancient Maya Wisdom and Knowledge is just the tip of the iceberg.

Curse forever those Spanish conquistadors who tried to destroy all of our books and history which belonged to the next world's generations.

This information, this KNOWLEDGE exists and is available always to those who are really willing to study it.

Our life is not what you saw in the movie Apocalypse! It never had happened this way in Chichen Itza in my lifetime. It is wrong how they portrayed us; we are noble, beautiful, kind-hearted people.

Sacrifices were very rare and done in most difficult, exceptional situations such as droughts. Special drugs were used. It was our way of sending our best people as messengers to God for help.

Misunderstanding or lack of knowledge about our culture and history is not the way to create something from your own mind, and turn it into public display trying to make money on the energy emanating from fear, blood and suffering. Fear was introduced to society artificially as an instrument of manipulation, and it prevented the development of new consciousness and enlightenment. Shame on those who used our Holy pyramid for this purpose and tried to cast a shadow on my pure temple in return. They should fix this mistake to avoid karma punishment.

The Pyramid was always a very special place for the meetings with God and Spirits. It was a House of Souls. It was our Big, Perfect Crystal. It was my home and my place of work.

Creativity is the only one important product on Earth and the reason for people to be here. Those talented producers who will create a great movie about us in the next three years will receive our special blessing.

This Pyramid is an important part of our Galactic structure as an energy and information exchange between the Earth and the Cosmos.

It will be nice to continue to perform rituals with a Priest in it, who will connect people with the God. SNAKE, EAGLE, ANUBIS and JAGUAR energy should be present at special celebration time.

Soon will be the beginning of a new Katun and Baktun time cycles.

Difficult times of changes are starting now. The planet and the world around us are overwhelmed by the side effect of huge population and in need of rest. Please stop expanding your family by bringing new spirits to the Earth for the next seven years. You will learn that it will help your family and you personally dramatically. Don't let outside fear take control over your inner voice and your own spirit. Stay in Harmony. We have many lives. Remember that your guardian angel's spiritual assistance is always near to support you.

Creativity and Love will help your Spirit be strong and survive the Time of Big Changes and proceed to the higher stage of evolution.

PRIEST JAGUAR, MAGICIAN.

Conclusion:

I think the Spirit body looks like a 3-D hologram, with some sort of crystal-like appearance. For some reason, I always see my Spirit as a perfect, strong crystal, as perfect as a diamond.

Our body is covered with an energy field, which is actually a matrix, a plan of the body structure. Inside our body there are over a million biochemical changes occurring every second. Our body is in constant changes. This plan around the body controls its functions and re-builds everything according to that plan. Maybe this energy field structure is responsible for our thinking process and consciousness. The thinking brain can only exist on biochemical or at the molecular and atom levels, where the possibility of "containers" for the consciousness on the level of elemental particles and their fields may exist. The Biofield is an ideal environment for *fluctuation*, which are holograms. It is possible to say that the biofield is actually a multi-component hologram. This way all of the person's life experiences – all his words, thoughts, words he ever said or someone said to him, what he saw, what he felt, all of his emotions – everything is preserved in that biofield in the form of holograms. These sets of holograms together form a kind of crystal, which we could name Soul or Spirit. (You will find more about our Spirit's characteristics at the end of the book Re-birth of an Atlantean Queen in Scientific Interpretations section – Discovery of biofield)

In addition, I am sure the crystals' structure of the Spirit is the best to collect and save information from one lifetime to the next. The same as with any kind of information, to preserve it on the real crystals is much better than using something like CDs, DVDs or paper.

I am thinking now that when people travel through the Universe in their dreams, what we call here, an "astral body" is actually this crystal made from sets of many hologram components. It is interesting that the body of the person, who left with visitors from another planet to see their world, did not exist in time and space. Maybe it is transformed into the field structure, because this is the only way of entering the world of the field forms.

(Please see the Kukulcan book; where I described, in my many dreams, my connection with creatures from the Universe, and while I am myself, my body turns into the wave-field structure.)

In the dream below, I tried to describe the crystallization process of my body as a preparation for space travel.

Dream # 41. A Gray Dumb-Bell in the Head, September 4, 1991, (see, "The Re-birth of an Atlantean Queen", by Julia SvadiHatra).
I had not fallen asleep deeply yet, I still remember myself, when some substance of gray color entered my head from both sides and started to crystallize inside it. It was not a pipe, the whole thing was filled in, crystallized all at once, and it was fitting very well...

However, when a person returns to our reality, to our world, that "plan structure around the body" shows amazing capabilities for analyzing and collecting components and for regeneration; returning these components into their previous structure, not only at the body level, but also at the level of consciousness and emotions.

Maybe while we are here on Earth, in the form of physical bodies, we are collecting some experiences into this energy field, crystal structure, named Soul or Spirit. After the biological body dies, we fly toward the

Universe Consciousness with all of these new qualities that we accumulated during our life as a human in the physical, materialistic world, where the field-form from Space just cannot develop at all.

Table of Common Characteristics

Common things in life; characters, habits, looks, interests, activities in the lives of the four people, who lived from 70 years, to 2 thousand and 10 thousand years apart from each other.

CHARACTERISTICS	AMELIA EARHART	JULIA SVADI HATRA	MAYA PRIEST	QUEEN OF ATLANTIS
Healing & Medicine	Yes	Yes	Yes	Yes
Basketball	Yes	Yes	Yes	No
Biology, agriculture, herbal plants	Yes	Yes	Yes	Possible
Math	Yes	Yes	Yes	Yes
Maps; land & sky	Yes	Yes	Yes	Possible
Airplanes, aviation, travel in space	Yes	Yes	Yes	Yes
Black hairy creatures *"Jabberwocky"*	Yes	Yes	Yes	
Love stars, addiction to the sky	Yes	Yes	Yes	Yes
Can't drink tea, coffee	Yes	Yes		
Tomato Juice	Yes	Yes		
Lougheed as an airplane & nurse's last name	Yes	Yes		
Hart and Hatra	Yes	Yes		
Flower named Amelia Jasmine Rose Lily	Yes	Yes		Possible
Twin trees with couples' names	Yes	Yes		
Leadership	Yes	Yes	Yes	Yes
High responsibility	Yes	Yes	Yes	Yes
Strength of character, brave nature	Yes	Yes	Yes	Yes
Responsible for the well-being of her people, society community	Yes	Yes	Yes	Yes
Hunting	Yes	Yes	Yes	
Ghost, Atchison "Most Ghostly Town in USA"	Yes	Yes	Yes	

The Priest

CHARACTERISTICS	AMELIA EARHART	JULIA SVADI HATRA	MAYA PRIEST	QUEEN OF ATLANTIS
Curse	Yes	Yes	Yes	
Importance of numbers	Yes	Yes	Yes	Yes
Persistence and perseverance	Yes	Yes	Yes	Yes
Lots of followers, pioneers	Yes	Yes	Yes	Yes
Studying, sciences	Yes	Yes	Yes	Yes
Open new freedom and new possibilities	Yes	Yes		
Drowning	Yes	Yes	Unknown	Possible
Problems with own children	Yes	Yes	Yes	Yes
Worker in charge of children, teaching	Yes	Yes	Yes	
Big "ego"	Yes	No	Yes	No
Adoring Asia – Japan, China	Yes	Yes	Unknown	Yes
Fine Arts	Yes	Yes	Yes	Yes
Physics, studies the sounds of the rocks, energy, transportation	Yes	Yes	Yes	Yes
Music, sounds	Yes	Yes	Yes	Unknown
Poetry	Yes	Yes	Unknown	
Chemistry	Yes	Yes	Possible	
Zoology	Yes	Yes	Possible	
Pacifist	Yes	Yes	Unknown	Yes
Supreme intelligence	Yes	Yes	Yes	Yes
Same facial features	Yes	Yes	No	Yes
Deeply spiritual	Yes	Yes	Yes	Yes
Creativity	Yes	Yes	Yes	Yes
True love	Yes	Yes	Possible	Yes
Thick hair	Yes	Yes	Yes	Yes
Extensive travel	Yes	Yes	Possible	Possible
Martial Arts, tomboy	Yes	Yes	Yes	NO
Fear of "lost for ever"	Yes	Yes		
Younger sister	Yes	Yes		
Angry black dog	Yes	Yes		
Someone named Mary	Yes	Yes		
Girlfriends named Laura in school	Yes	Yes		

CHARACTERISTICS	AMELIA EARHART	JULIA SVADI HATRA	MAYA PRIEST	QUEEN OF ATLANTIS
"Extreme" people in extreme situations	Yes	Yes	Yes	Yes
Pilot shirt, similar clothing	Yes	Yes		
Astrology	Unknown	Yes	Yes	Yes
Jaguar skin, or print clothes		Yes	Yes	
Tortoise (turtle)		Yes	Yes	
White jaguar		Yes	Yes	
Connection with the Goddess, meeting with God		Yes	Yes	Yes
Word Caracol		Yes	Yes	
Word *Equinox* talking in ancient Maya		Yes	Yes	
Priesthood, priest's connection		Yes	Yes	Yes
Intuition, predictions	Yes	Yes	Yes	Yes
Masks		Yes	Yes	
Sacrifices		Yes	Yes	
Aztec God Xochipilli		Yes	Yes	
Addiction to crystals, growing crystals, diamonds, museums, factories		Yes	Yes	Yes
Playing the same "Rock from the past"		Yes	Yes	
Laser, X-ray technology, studied seeds		Yes	Yes	Yes
Book opening up like an accordion, website moving bar, business plan		Yes	Yes	
Spirit support		Yes	Yes	
Big, tall people		Yes	Yes	Yes
Materialization, teleportation, moving objects		Yes		Yes

I recognize now that I am lucky in life, because I had the rare possibility to see the chain of my past lives, the echoes from my past, and make adjustments to my future, spiritual development.

These four people had the same Spirit, which was transferred from the life of one person to the next and to the next. Skills, habits, experience, and knowledge accumulated in the Spirit holographic crystal are transferred with the Spirit to the next newborn person as an inheritance from all of his past lives. This is the chain of lives of people who carried the same Spirit. The Spirit of the people is ETERNAL.

Sources

1. *Maya calendars - Yukatek Maya.* From Wikipedia, the free encyclopedia.

2. *An archaeological study of chirped echo from the Mayan pyramid of Kukulcan at Chichen Itza* by David Lubman.

3. The Miracle Man: The Life Story of João de Deus, *by* Robert Pellegrino-Ostrich. Extracted from his book Published in 1997, ©1997/1998 All Rights Reserved.

4. http://www.crystalinks.com/gordianknot.html

5. Wikipedia: http://en.wikipedia.org/wiki/Knot_theory

6. Akiane Kramarik http://www.artakiane.com) http://www.tagtele.com/videos/voir/19214/1/Connie

7. The numbers 5, 8 and 13 belong to the Gibonacci sequence, defining phi. Daniel Pinchbeck, 2012 The return of Quetzalcoatl.

8. Genady Belimov, “Soul and Intelligence of the Plants”, TD 2005.

9. Ancient America: flight in time and prostransive. Mezoamerika, (excerpts from the book by GG Ershovoy. Un-copyrighted@Sam, 2003-2006).

Testimonials

Reading your book but I am crying so much reading I can hardly read it. Your book resonates so much with me, so much emotions it brings up. You put your heart in this book to touch the hearts of the readers.
Buryl Payne.

I really do think from what I wrote that you are an amazing woman, someone that comes along once in a life time. You are a real live Goddess! Most priceless alive human on the planet at our time. I really mean it is Incredible! Your outlook on life, philosophy and spiritual beliefs are outstanding and intriguing. Your dreams are very smart, unusual, bright and full of dynamic. It attracts like a magnet to read your wise book. Intelligence far beyond normal. What is your IQ?
Henry D.

Best book to take to the banker!
It will never be boring to read it over and over again for many years!
Your book like a jewelry box for me, which if you would open it; you would be astonished seeing the flush of rare, magic multicolored things inside it. You are AVATAR who opened this rare knowledge to all of us.
hurrican888

I dreamed about you last night and the overall theme was: connected by the light and flying through space.... it made me very happy, I have had many past lives, also in Atlantis, Egypt etc., so no doubt we know each other.
Marianne Notschaele-den Boer www.vorigelevens.nl

Wow! I guess I discovered real treasure here!
silvercrystall

That is so wonderful, and you should be so very proud of yourself. Just think of the impact that you can have on the lives of others through your book...opening up their minds, their spirituality, their soul, and their current lives!!!!!!"
Christopher M.

Afraid to die? Just read front page of that website!
http://www.ameliareborn.com/
and you will never afraid again! Never! Can't wait to read whole book... Amazing!
Miracleforest

Got this weekend your book in the hand. Even touching the book gave me already trills.
I have been reading several parts of it. It is more than amazing. Your statement that 'spirit is eternal' is well emphasized and believable. Your contribution to testify from the invisible world will bring back a lot of people to live a sound faith driven life. You know that you are abundantly blessed, set-apart and might fully used to serve as a priest.
It was already written by the prophet Hosea: (free quote) 'My people (says Yahweh) are destroyed for lack of knowledge.' He blames the priests for it as it is their task to instruct the people and that during that period priests neglected that and lived a shameful decadent life, not caring for the common man.
Now you are here, bringing the knowledge that can save the people from destruction. That's exactly why your speech, book(s) and video(s) should be spread rapidly all over the world in many languages. Sure a giant enterprise and of course you will persevere.
Reading your book my reverence is increasing strongly for you being out there as a living testimonial of the Spirit world. Many mediums, psychics etc. tried to approach me in vain the last 20-yrs, as none of them were pure and badly wired with the parallel world. Now

finally there is you! The living model of faith, hope, love, creativity and beauty. Blessed are you that brings peace of mind instead of fear. I will order 10 copies of the book to hand over to friends. Also to my granddaughter, who was thrilled after reading the back cover.

Alfons Ven
EVOLUTION VISION foundation
Deviser of the 28-day cure.
e-mail: info@alfonsven.com
www.slideshare.net/alfonsven

Where to order the book or CDs:

For any information, please visit the website:
http://www.ameliareborn.com/
www.ameliareborn.com

Or contact me at:
contact@ameliareborn.com

YOU TUBE
amelia reborn
2012 Maya Priest

To buy this or any of Julia SvadiHatra's five books on line, please visit Amazon.com, BarnesandNobles.com, Borders.com or ChapterIndigo.com and write the title of your choice in the "search window".

CDs – available for purchase at
www.ameliareborn.com

1. Di Cherry introduction to past life readings, hypnosis.
2. Reading Priest

Read More...

In the book, "**WHO IS CHAK MOL?**" you will find who the Ancient Priest meets in Chichen Itza! Guess who it was? A Mexican hero, Chak Mol! You will find out who he was; where he came from before arriving in Mexico and Chichen Itza and even who his mother was! He was a giant Atlantean man! You will find out where he lived and where he played in Chichen Itza.

In the book, "**KUKULCAN**" an Ancient Maya Priest comes to you through thousands of years and giving rare knowledge what you can expect after your own death. All people will live in Spirit world between lives. The spirit world is full of amazing colors, lights, dynamics speed and magic things which do not exist in our world. Travel in Time? Teleportation? Meeting with Kukulcan-Quetzalcoatl. Who is he? From where GIANTS come on Earth? Why people build pyramids? Do we live in the Past or in the Future?

In the book, "**AMELIA REBORN?**" Amelia is talking to us. Astonishing secrets are revealed. Was Amelia meant to die according to some "secret plan"? Through the author's past life experience, Amelia is able to describe the last minutes before her death, how she enters Heaven. Why was she lost? Why is it impossibly difficult to find her? Is it a curse by ancient Egyptian or Mexican spirits on those who are "playing games" around Amelia's disappearance?

What is common between Amelia and the Ancient Priest of Chichen Itza?
In this book you will also find details of Amelia's SPIRIT JOURNEY from her life in Ancient Egypt. Did Amelia belong to a royal family of Ancient Egypt or was she a Priestess there? A unique Egypt's ancient initiation

ceremony of a Goddess, meeting with Egyptian Goddesses and magic of the Holy Spirit of Bast, the Royal Cat Goddess, intriguing Anubis, communication with an Ancient Priest & Pharaoh, swimming in the efir oils, present to the Great Cheops pyramid, ancient ritual inside the tomb, talking to mummies, GIANT Pharaohs... are all in this truly Mysterious Magic Egypt.

In the book, "**THE REBIRTH OF AN ATLANTEAN QUEEN**" you will find the complete story about the Spirit Journey of Amelia and all her other past lives as a Priest of Chichen Itza, an Atlantean Queen, Ancient Egyptian royal Priestess, Julia Svadihatra and even one future life. This big book contains all 4 books we just mentioned: Priest, Who is Chak Mol, Amelia Reborn, Kukulcan and an additional chapter: The Rebirth of an Atlantean Queen about life in Atlantis. Was Amelia an Atlantean Queen in her past life? Did she carry with her secrets of the crystal pyramid and how to re-ignite its energy? In this book Amelia's Spirit went back to her past life in Atlantis and her abilities began to emerge in this life time in a new re-born person!

Enjoy reading.

Exclusive editor of all 5 books:
Roxane Christ, www.1steditor.biz

Appendix

The sure way to evolve from now on into a better self!

Alfons Ven, an Engineer, turned healer out of necessity.

Alfons Ven devised a 28-day "Matrix Support Program" to evolve from now on "into a better self".
Giving everybody a chance to live a healthy and *victorious* life.

THE MATRIX OF TWELVE ASPECTS
It all started with a vision. How plants overcame their fear to be devoured, and were endowed with subtle invisible information to overcome and control it.
That insight evolved further into Twelve Aspects. (See figure below.)
Each Aspect covers specific regulating evolutionary patterns.
Alfons introduces these patterns onto pills giving readjusting instructions to man, in order to

- Clarify and be at peace with the past.
- Get better attuned with the Invisible.
- Discover and live the real, original you.
- Live a safe and well-balanced existence.
- Realize what you imagine.
- Unlock your personality.
- Boost your awareness.
- Free your spirit.
- Restore your soul.
- Heal your body and mind
- Evolve from now on into better.
- Reap the fruits of progress and growth.

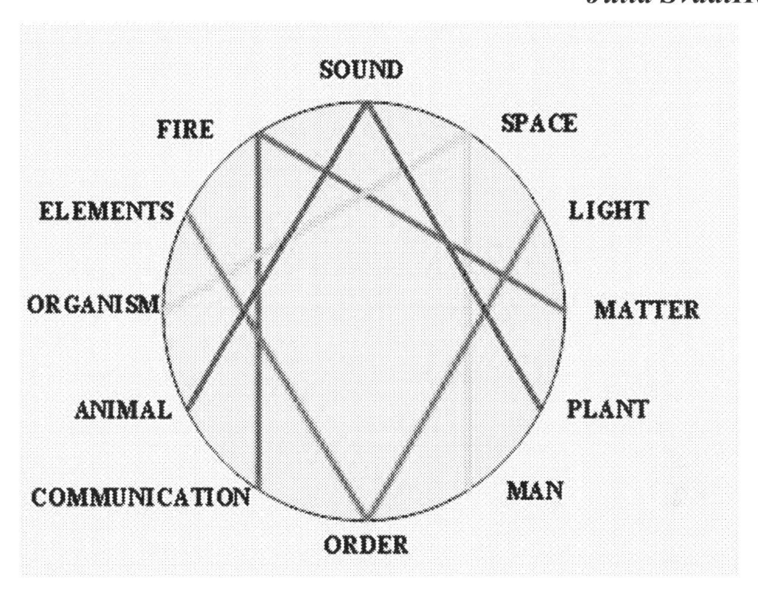

The conditions are simple:

- Just start with a "Matrix Support Program".
- Let it happen and rely on your *'automatic goal-striving, built-in regulating system'*.
- Respect your very best nature.
- Commit to good causes and realistic goals.
- Stay focused and grateful.
- Act swiftly when opportunity knocks.

The "Matrix Support Program" is inserted in a blister pack – easy to use. Over the 28-day program, a few little sugar pills are taken. It's that simple. The pills are inert. Meaning that no chemical substance has been added during their manufacturing. Therefore, there are no side effects, no possible overdose. Young and old – man and animal alike – can safely use them.
The patterns on the pills affect the *invisible* part of us and are not to be taken as a medicine in the literal or scientific sense.

Where to begin?

STEP-1
The Step-1-Program is equipped to deal with a wide range of problems – to clear up many hidden issues while readjusting your body as a whole. It's also an extensive grounding treatment. It assists in the constitutional upgrade and the rebalancing of the metabolism. It also facilitates the reintegration of the 'Twelve Aspects'. It has a deep restoring effect on the immune system.

STEP-2
If one feels that there are still some unresolved issues, it is recommended to state the issues in an e-mail. A personalized Step-2-Program can then be designed for your particular needs. This may be repeated to upgrade your functionality even more.

STEP-3
This Step is an invitation to progress and growth, to assist you further in the fine-tuning to the Twelve Aspects.

THE ALFONS VEN FOUNDATION
Has been helping people worldwide since 1996. Amazing testimonials of healing and changes of life for the better keep streaming in daily.
Whatever your issues are, whatever you tried before, the "Matrix Support Program" is always an asset.

Notes: Helpdesk: myriam@alfonsven.com or call: +31 30 233 3188
Website: www.alfonsven.com
Statement: The Alfons Ven Foundation is not affiliated with any *political, religious, esoteric, spiritual groups or organizations* whatsoever.